THE AFTERMATH OF REVOLUTION IN LATIN AMERICA

TULIO HALPERIN-DONGHI

Translated from the Spanish by Josephine de Bunsen

HARPER TORCHBOOKS

Harper & Row, Publishers
New York, Evanston, San Francisco, London

This book is available in hardcover
from Harper & Row, Publishers, Inc.

THE AFTERMATH OF REVOLUTION IN LATIN AMERICA.

Translated by Josephine de Bunsen.

First HARPER TORCHBOOK edition published 1973.

LIBRARY OF CONGRESS CATALOG CARD NUMBER: 72–83822

STANDARD BOOK NUMBER: 06–131711–X (PAPERBACK)

STANDARD BOOK NUMBER: 06–136097–X (HARDCOVER)

Designed by Ann Scrimgeour

CONTENTS

INTRODUCTION

In his later years the Argentine writer and statesman Domingo Faustino Sarmiento liked to compare the disconcerting trajectory covered by Latin America from the time of the declaration of independence until the middle of the nineteenth century with the forty years' wandering of the Israelites in the desert. Since he would hardly have accepted as a justification of adversity its supposed penitential and purificational role, in stressing this comparison he probably wished to add solemnity to his assertion that these years had been wasted.

Many of the protagonists of the period and particularly those who had to suffer its brutal vicissitudes without even aspiring to influence the course of events would probably have agreed with his bitter diagnosis. From the moment, during the wars for independence, that the embattled revolutionary governments began to use the threat of implacable reprisals against the defeated as a means of obtaining the active support of their people, it began to become apparent that the somewhat blind optimism of 1810 had completely disappeared and that fear, rather than hope, dominated the vision of a future being forged in revolution and war.

The postwar period brought new occasions for disquiet, justified or otherwise. It is easy now for us to prescribe the attitude which should have been adopted at the time. But not only is such second-guessing irrelevant, it leads us to forget that the attitude was inherent to the event itself.

Although the value of contemporary diagnoses is undeniable, they gave rise, almost always, to very inexact forecasts. Those who lived in that tormented period were impressed by the perpetual instability that seemed to pervade more than politics. Fear that this instability would result in the eventual dissolution of the few cohesive elements which had survived the revolution dominated their view of the shape of things to come. Today it is the maddening stability of the basic elements of life during the period which first impresses us as we begin our studies of the facts of the period.

Rather than enumerate the causes of an impending sociopolitical crisis, which never arrived, this study will seek to discover why the changes, which those who established independence thought would be immediate, were delayed almost fifty years. Politicians used all their originality throughout this span in endeavoring to give coherence and stability to the new order. It is precisely to understanding their efforts and this epoch that this book is dedicated.

1

THE HERITAGE OF WAR

Spanish America achieved its independence through war, and it was war which, in one way or another, left its mark upon the whole of this vast region. War was responsible, in the first place, for the direct destruction of material wealth, although this alone was not enough decisively to change the Latin American scene, and secondly and indirectly for a far more widespread destruction, to which the inundated silver mines of Mexico, the abandoned haciendas of the Peruvian coast and the remoter corners of Venezuela, and the chronic state of hunger and civil war in certain areas of the Río de la Plate all bore witness. It is not, however, always easy to measure the extent to which the war was responsible for those scenes of desolation: all the changes which accompanied independence contributed to a varying extent. Those whose fortune it was to live in the difficult period which succeeded the wars of independence chose to regard the heritage of war primarily as a change of climate which seemed to affect the entire collective way of life in Spanish America, namely, was the institution of violence as an ever-present menace, only too apparent in the insecurity alike of men and objects in the towns and on the roads.

A vast amount of evidence is readily available concerning the perils awaiting the traveler in the new Spanish America, so different from the submissive continent of pre-1810, whose passive acceptance of the Spanish king's authority was retrospectively exaggerated as well as regarded as positive. Upon closer examination it becomes apparent that the threat was most prevalent in ports and large towns where there were then, as earlier, the greatest number of vagabonds prepared to steal when occasion arose. In Valparaíso (Chile), the friends of the recently widowed María Graham disapproved of her decision to settle alone in a small house in the district of Almendral, for it was only too well known that no house was safe there.[1] There, as in Santiago, Buenos Aires, and Mexico, the streets were no safer than the houses. This lack of safety extended even to some of the well-used highways, as in Mexico, and above all to those (such as the road to Pasco in Peru) which tempted the desperately needy population with the hope of obtaining exceptional spoils. On the outskirts of the towns the same insecurity was apparent. Robber bands outside Lima and criminals outside Buenos Aires had to be firmly repressed even at the time of the revolution itself. But it would be dangerous to generalize, and it should be remembered that the enumeration of perils was a traditional narrative device among the writers of traveler's tales.

In October 1844 José Manuel Restrepo, the verbose chronicler of Nueva Granada, was horrified to learn of an unusual event: the Magdalena mail had been assaulted. He attributed it possibly to "negligence on the part of its conductors, who trusted too far to the morality of our people." Are we then to deplore the passing of a blessed age in which it was possible to walk "alone through the woods and deserts, laden with gold and silver with no other weapon than a machete"?[2] The situation lasted until 1844 and was not as exceptional in Spanish America as Restrepo appears to have thought. John Miers describes his experiences in Chile in almost identical words, saying that "a person may travel over all parts of the countryside without the least fear of robbery," although here too the most important road in the country, that joining Santiago and Valparaíso, was reputedly unsafe. Even in this context, however, Miers, a British would-be miner and industrialist, stated that he met with no misadventure in spite of the fact that he used to travel "alone once or twice a week from Concón to Valparaíso, carrying much money about me, reaching home long after dark."[3]

It is interesting to note another common element in the Chilean and Nueva Granada incidents. In the Chilean countryside the few violent robberies were mostly committed by "the renegade sons of

[1] María Graham, *Diario de una residencia en Chile* (Madrid, 1916), p. 157.

[2] J. M. Restrepo, *Diario político y militar*, October 7, 1844, III (Bogotá, 1954): 393.

[3] J. Miers, *Travels in Chile and La Plata*, II (London, 1826): 247.

hacendados," whereas in Nueva Granada, in the episode cited by Restrepo, there were doubts "concerning certain of the notables of the district." In contrast to the urban and suburban robberies committed by criminals, the few episodes which disturbed the unexpectedly solid rural order were due to socially predominant people who, in taking to open banditry, merely carried the extreme attitudes current in the defense of that very order one step further. William MacCann, who visited the province of Buenos Aires, Argentina, during the height of the Rosista period, deduced that the heads of the rural army and the local justices of the peace were a far greater hazard to contend with than the delinquents, and his conclusion is similar to those of many other travelers of the time.[4] Twenty years earlier W. B. Beaumont described more circumstantially his suspicions that the local police and justice in the Argentine province of Entre Ríos had taken to legalized banditry, and Miers himself, who had vehemently described the exceptional safety enjoyed by people and property alike in the Chilean countryside, remarked that district judges were given to the extortion of their unfortunate prisoners and overinclined to protect thieves.[5] He also stated that *hacendados* were conspicuously excluded from this arbitrary victimization and that the officials were "respectful and obsequious" to them in exchange for small favors. That this arbitrary behavior was nothing new is overwhelmingly apparent in the documents of the colonial period, but there is one important difference: after independence illegality was far more frequently accompanied by violence, or the threat thereof, than formerly. This was one of the many, almost inevitable consequences of a war which had vastly increased the number of men under arms, not only for offensive purposes, but also to support the administrative apparatus. It was this support which brought about militarization of the administration, to a varied but always considerable degree.

The nature of the wars of independence made armed support necessary. In what was essentially civil war, neither the supporters of the new order nor those of the old could rely implicitly on the obedience of the people; furthermore, the endemic financial weak-

[4] W. MacCann, *Viaje a caballo* (*Buenos Aires,* 1939), p. 120.
[5] Miers, *Travels,* II: 146–148.

ness of the different political factions obliged them to resort to the wealth of private individuals who were reluctant to relinquish it. Militarization had two main consequences during the period of the war itself: first, it increased the political power of the army and its leaders, both because war was the first commitment of the new states and because it was expedient to use a military organization for administrative purposes at a time when financial and human resources were at their lowest; the second and more subtle consequence being the emergence of a military dimension in the activities of the local authorities, linked to the growing need for coercion over the administered populations. The picture was still further complicated by the presence of local groups of militia, dating from prerevolutionary times, which acquired great significance in certain areas. As for the army itself, it was in some regions a direct offshoot of the royalist army, and hence endowed with a complex and institutional structure, while in others it stemmed from revolution and improvisation. In other words, while the character of public life in Spanish America became militarized, the military institutions tended to reflect the frequently contradictory complexities of postrevolutionary Spanish America. In order to examine the consequences of militarization, the varying context provided by the new nations must be taken into account.

Militarization in Mexico reflected the peculiarities of the country's prerevolutionary and postrevolutionary history. The fact that Bourbon Spain felt the northern frontiers of its Spanish American empire to be badly threatened was responsible, during the second half of the eighteenth century, for the emergence of a military organization which gave its officers a privileged position in Mexican society. Bearing in mind this situation and the conclusions of Lyle McAlister, Woodrow Borah has suggested that the frequently ill-defined Spanish American militarism, which most Spanish American scholars date as postrevolutionary, could well have originated during colonial times.[6] In any case, the characteristics

---

[6] W. Borah, "Colonial Institutions and Contemporary Latin America: Political and Economic Life," *Hispanic American Historical Review*, vol. XLIII, no. 3 (August, 1963): pp. 371–379.

of the Mexican wars of independence confirmed and intensified a tendency which had already made its appearance in the late 1700s.

The Mexican Revolution, begun by Hidalgo and continued by Morelos, was, in fact, the most plebeian of the Spanish American revolutions of 1810. Precisely for this reason—in a continent where fears of a takeover by the Indian population were still frequent by the middle of the nineteenth century—it roused the opposition of entire sectors of society. Spaniard and Creole alike united, as privileged members of society, against that sector which the colonial order had placed lowest in the hierarchy. It was only after 1815, when the danger of such a plebeian uprising was reduced, that the unity of the resisting forces began to disintegrate, but it was, above all, political events in Spain which finally brought the situation to a head. The Spanish liberal revolution of 1820 gave the more enlightened Creoles a chance to speak, and its decidedly innovational character provoked the disaffection of other Mexican political sectors; both groups joined forces to separate Mexico from a Spain which had ceased to exercise a conservative influence.

The army, stronger and more vigorous after the struggle against revolution, was an essential component of the new Mexico. Although unable to impose a decidedly conservative political trend (with which, from the very beginning, it sympathized less than had been expected and to which it became progressively less sympathetic as the revolutionary leaders joined its ranks), it nonetheless weighed heavily in establishing the political tendencies of the country, whether conservative or liberal. Its privileges, which then, as in colonial times, included a special tribunal for the military, and its expenses, which accounted for more than half the annual national budget, had to be tolerated by those in power. The alliance of the army with the conservatives was not based on the social origin or the ideological inclinations of its officers but came about only after the liberals were rash enough to challenge its privileged status in 1833. Within the army officers of the upper classes consorted with others who, under the old order, would not have had access to such positions. While some originated in the rank and file of the revolution, such as Guadalupe Victoria and

Vicente Guerrero, others had attained promotion in the royalist army, where the necessities of war had attenuated exclusion based on caste differences.

The presence in the Mexican political setup of the army as a deciding factor, wielding its power to further its own corporative interests, was a source of dissatisfaction to many apart from the politicians who were directly affected thereby, and in the 1820s an attempt was made to curb its strength by means of provincial militias. Unfortunately, the results of this experiment eventually alarmed even its most enthusiastic supporters. They continually threatened to become the private armies of locally influential figures, opening up the prospect of dissolving internal order and leading to terrible caste war. This was alarming even to the liberals who still remembered with distaste the revolution of Hidalgo (even Lorenzo de Zavala, one of the less moderate liberals, who disfavorably compared the badly armed native followers of Hidalgo with the brilliant professional army whose backing made Iturbide's pronunciamiento a much more respectable political enterprise).[7] But although the militia proved even more dangerous than the regular army, Zavala and the more moderate Mora proposed reorganizing them on the basis of property, arguing that a militia organized and paid for by the landowners would not only reduce military expenditure but would definitely place military strength at the service of social order rather than costly political adventure.[8]

This solution was obviously inapplicable in Mexico, where the army was strong enough to prevent the development of any potential rival, but even elsewhere it eventually became apparent that its political expediency was counterbalanced by inefficiency in battle. This was particularly evident in Venezuela when the Conservative Republic which emerged in 1830 after the division of Gran Colombia made an effort to reduce further the size of the regular army, which already comprised only about 2,500 men. Páez, the *llanero* chief who during the greater part of the Gran Colombia

[7] L. de Zavala, *Ensayo,* I: 117–118; discussed in C. A. Hale, *Mexican Liberalism* (New Haven, 1968), p. 26.

[8] Hale, *Mexican Liberalism,* p. 143.

wars of independence held the Venezuelan rear guard for Bolívar, felt very little sympathy for the Venezuelan military who had accompanied the armies of independence to Nueva Granada, Quito, and Peru and who became nostalgic for the larger Gran Colombian scene after their return to Venezuela. However, only when the army rebelled against his civilian successor, Dr. José Maria Vargas, was Páez able to strike a decisive blow by reducing the regular army even further (although it was supposed to comprise 1,000 men, it was made up of only 800 in 1838 and somewhat fewer than 500 in 1842); moreover, the fortress of Puerto Cabello, which the revolutionaries of 1835 had hoped to make their center, was demolished. Simultaneously, in 1836 the organization of the militia was drastically revised. Active service was limited to those who could buy their own uniforms, arms, and munitions, and the remainder of those fit to serve were relegated to the reserve. Although the active militia—which recruited only those who had something to lose—played a decisive role in the victory over the Liberal uprising of 1846–1847, its predominant position within the Venezuelan military structure was not to last. In 1848 a new president, José Tadeo Monagas, who had taken part in the 1835 rebellion and subsequently made his peace with Páez, decided to rid himself of the latter and of parliament with one stroke. To achieve his end, he resuscitated the reserve militia, giving it leaders taken to a great extent from among the veterans of the Gran Colombia campaigns and soldiers recruited "from the dregs of the populace," and therewith obtained an easy victory over the inert parliament which had been imprudent enough to attempt to bring the new president to justice.[9] At this juncture, both the deliberately weakened army and the active militia revealed their basic military incapacity. The fact was that the latter, which granted the monopoly of force to the landowners, could offer at best but a passive guarantee of stability for an already stable conservative government and, even during the golden age of Conservative Venezuela, could give no more than additional security to a regime whose real strength—as it boasted—lay in the

[9] Restrepo, *Diario,* March 4, 1848, III: 543.

reasoned and unanimous support of public opinion. Its limitations are easily appreciable. Made up of men who had, by definition, a vested interest in maintaining peace, it would not take part in subversive activities and might assist in subduing relatively weak rebel centers, but its pacific inclinations prevented it from acting efficaciously in the event of a prolonged civil war. In Venezuela its failure was that of the entire Conservative Restoration, which managed only briefly to impose a superficial calm on the country, more ravaged than any other in Spanish America by the struggle for independence. Páez, and together with him many veterans to whom war had given access to the privileged governing class of Conservative Venezuela, could consider war and adventure definitely a thing of the past—in Páez's case a past during which he had risen from *llanero* foreman to general, president, and a great landowner in independent Venezuela—but the lasting effects of the destruction of social discipline in town and country alike made the organization of an active militia in which only the officers would be men of property too dangerous for the existing order.

The excess of veteran army officers with whom the Conservative regime did not quite know what to do added to the potential for instability. Struck from the payroll after the uprising of 1835, the greater part were restored to it again at the beginning of the following decade, and while playing no further part in the balance of military power, since the Conservatives dispensed with their services, they were yet available to subvert it.

It was not only war which was responsible for the Venezuelan chaos. The transformation of the export economy, by which cocoa and plantation agriculture lost their primacy, the consequent increase of sharecropping, the rise of an urban sector whose strength lay in commerce and credit to important positions within the Venezuelan economy—all contributed to the downfall of the landowning class who alone would have made the militia both efficient as a defense weapon and immune to the temptations of political adventure.[10]

[10] E. Gilmore, *Caudillism and Militarism* (Athens, Ohio, 1964), pp. 112–114, 135 ff.

The landowner-controlled militia was to work more effectively within a more solidly conservative context, such as Nueva Granada or Chile. Restrepo's alarmed account of the uprisings of 1839–1841 reveals a sequence of events which might be regarded as typical. In Pasto, where the abolition of convents marked the beginning of the disturbances, the governor decided to withdraw to the veterans' barracks and parley with the rebels, since he had only 70 regular soldiers and officers with whom to face 3,000 rebels. In October 1840 a retired colonel, notorious for his subversive activities, found no difficulty in seizing the veterans' headquarters in Medellín, which were only lightly guarded, and in between these two episodes Popayán successfully quelled a threat of rebellion, but only because "youth and the militia hastened to take up arms," since in Popayán too "there were few veteran troops." In all three cases the veteran army was either overwhelmed or inhibited from action, and in the three instances in which the government, so ill defended by an army apparently unable to defend itself, won the day, it was almost invariably because the militia were brought into action. Such was the case in the south, in Antioquia and in Bogotá.

In defending the existing order from civil war and fighting rebels, the militia was defending property rather than government, but the very order it sought to preserve had its enemies. In Pasto, the stronghold of fierce royalist resistance during the wars of independence, war was inevitable. According to Restrepo, "not the inhabitants of the city who have something to lose" but "the Indians and other miserable wretches who own nothing . . . who by means of war earn the right daily to eat the meat of the cattle they steal" made war unavoidable "while means for subsistence survive." In the upper Cauca valley preventive rules for the repression of the freed black slaves were hastily drawn up when "bandits" proclaimed their liberation following the precedent set by the leaders of the recently suppressed uprising.[11] The existing order was aware of its enemies, but the outcome of the conflict (in which the regular army was swayed primarily by the leaders grown up in its ranks, both on the royalist and on the insurrectionist

[11] Restrepo, *Diario,* III: 136–138, 155, 166, 189, 348.

sides) shows that those enemies were less powerful than the partisans of the status quo. Their strength and cohesion was derived, rather than from the political and military superiority of the government, from the social structure of Nueva Granada itself. Less affected by a war in which it had been less active than Venezuela and, again, economically archaic in contrast to dynamic postrevolutionary Venezuela, the social structures which Nueva Granada inherited from colonial times remained almost intact and supplied the solid basis for the militarily improvised but considerably effective resistance to all attempts violently to overthrow its rigid order.

The vigor of the traditional social structure limited the scope of revolutionary and postrevolutionary militarization. In Nueva Granada the regular army rapidly declined in importance. During the Gran Colombia period, the majority of its officers were Venezuelan—a disparity which was not repeated for the rank and file—and subsequently the greater part of them, compromised by their support of the Bolívar dictatorship and that of Urdaneta, or wishing perhaps to continue their careers in more propitious surroundings, left Nueva Granada, whose officer corps consequently became smaller than that of Venezuela itself, in spite of the fact that subsequent efforts to reduce the size of the army in the former country were not as successful as in the latter.[12] While the Venezuelan army accounted for 21.5 percent of the annual budget in 1842–1843, in Colombia it accounted for 50 percent and considerably more if expenses classified as financial, mainly pertaining to military back debts, are taken into account. It is also suggestive that until after the middle of the nineteenth century all the Colombian presidents were military men with the sole exception of Márquez, who did not complete his term of office and was replaced by General Herrán. The reason for this preference is noted by Restrepo, who comments with regard to the 1845 elections: "Dr. Rufino Cuervo will not be chosen, we think, because everybody is persuaded that a civilian cannot hold his own among us and that the military would pull him down."

Although the army was possibly as influential in Nueva Granada

[12] Gilmore, *Caudillism*, p. 141.

as in Venezuela, it exerted its influence in quite different ways. There, too, there were officers of low origin who tried to cash in politically on their influence with the troops, the most celebrated case, though not the only one, being that of General José María Obando, the "patriot of 1821" who carved out a career for himself in the royalist army until two years after the liberation of Nueva Granada by Bolívar and who subsequently gathered a following in Pasto thanks to the moderation he eventually displayed in the final repression of this royalist stronghold. After crusading against the ecclesiastic innovations of Márquez in 1839, he ended his career as the highest military paladin of liberalism. There were plenty of others, like the Gaitán brothers, who used the army to better their social positions. Major Domingo Gaitán placed the 180 soldiers under his command at the disposal of the rebels, and a younger brother, Alejandro, took with him "eight or ten companions, the most damnable in Bogotá," when defecting from the government forces. They and their elder brother, Colonel José María Gaitán, had, as Restrepo observed, "nothing to complain about in the government of their country; their temperaments are restless, and they wish to rise higher than their personal qualities and the humble environment from which the Republic has taken them allow."[13] In Nueva Granada, however, this behavior, rife among the officer corps elsewhere, was not only severely condemned but considered anomalous. In spite of the fact that the revolution implied an exceptionally violent upheaval both for the army and for the civilian population of Nueva Granada, it did not manage to disrupt the dominance of certain local families, firmly established already in colonial times. Thus the army strong man, together with Obando, was General Tomás Cipriano de Mosquera, son of the highest-ranking family of aristocratic Popayán and brother of the prelate who was to be archbishop of Bogotá after the wars of independence. While there is no doubt that the greater vigor of the prerevolutionary socioeconomic structure and the economic changes wrought by the revolution eventually made the army the instrument rather than the rival of the prerevolutionary elite, even

[13] Restrepo, *Diario,* III: 157–159, 384.

so the characteristics of revolutionary militarization played a decisive part in favoring this outcome of events.

After the suppression of the first revolutionary movements by the royalists, militarization in Nueva Granada was no longer a spontaneous process. After the liberation of Nueva Granada by Bolívar, it became apparent that the almost complete lack of spontaneity in the rebellion itself had prevented the emergence of military leaders risen from the ranks because their talent and capacity supplemented their social deficiencies. Consequently, when it became necessary to increase the size of the army, new officers had to be recruited far more frequently than elsewhere in Spanish America (excepting Chile, where the process of independence ran a very similar course) from the upper strata of that strictly stratified society.

But even military officers of unimpeachable pedigree were prone to the temptation to rid themselves of control by their social equals. Mosquera, whose political unruliness was the despair of the Conservatives before it became that of the Liberals to whom he finally transferred his allegiance, was a particularly good example, and it is hardly surprising that the traditionally predominant sector of society in Nueva Granada (which was able to retain its predominance better than elsewhere) should have used it slowly to undermine the political and military strength of the regular army. Although the process was not completed until the second half of the nineteenth century, the trend was apparent far earlier.

Chile is an even better example than Venezuela or Nueva Granada of a Conservative regime. Here too the intervention of the army in political affairs was eventually circumscribed, although this was a complex process. As in Nueva Granada, the first revolutionary army was destroyed together with the first revolution, and despite the fact that the subsequent liberation carried out from Argentina by San Martín with the assistance of refugee Chileans led by Bernardo O'Higgins was preceded and accompanied by spontaneous uprisings of far greater importance than in Nueva Granada, their potential effect on the equilibrium of the Chilean armed forces was nullified by suppression by the new regime of the popular leaders, which it considered insufficiently reliable. After independence the army was organized by the government in power and became characterized by increasing social and political conservatism, although it did not reflect the conventional pattern of national society as closely as in Nueva Granada. This was due to the fact that since colonial times the army had included many officers from the comparatively poor southern region, where the almost incessant war against the Araucanians created a sort of specialization in war. Even in Independent Chile this pattern was maintained for several decades. The officers were frequently related to one another, and this circumstance, together with their relative marginality, made them a threat to any political party which did not take them into account. The period of political disorder following the overthrow of O'Higgins in January 1823, which lasted until 1830, was marked by their increasing influence, mitigated only by the fact that they were as divided as the Chilean political elite.

Although the establishment of a government based exclusively on the professional army was thus rendered impossible, the political instability which characterized the whole period became so marked as a consequence of this situation that it became necessary to correct it. The decisive victory of one of the internal factions of the army, followed by a careful weeding out among the officers, lessened the temptation for further adventure, but it disappeared altogether only after the consolidation of a political order whose strength did not rely entirely on the military. One of the contributing factors to this consolidation was the creation of a civil guard or militia, with propertied officers, which, in 1837, played a decisive part in subduing the military rebellion responsible for the execution of Diego Portales, the politician who had been the master organizer of the Conservative Republic. From that time on, schemes for the violent overthrow of the current government arose less frequently from the army, although even in 1851 the renaissance of the Liberal opposition was accompanied by a similar resurgence of military opposition, subdued with difficulty by the Conservative government.

In Chile, as in Nueva Granada, the elimination of the army as an independent and at times critically dominant factor from the political scene was due less to the limited financial and human resources granted to it (characteristic primarily of the early thirties, since subsequently the ambitious external policy and the necessity of guarding the Indian frontier counteracted this tendency) than to the better achieved integration of the officer corps into a governing elite which, after elaborating a constitution ensuring itself a solid predominance, devoted itself to defending the same with a sincerity which there is no call to doubt. The originality of the Chilean solution lay in the fact that the governing body included a sector of professional politicians and administrators who, while not necessarily of a modest social background, did not owe their political preeminence to their family connections and who were the pivotal point of political stability between the army officers (two of whom, General Joaquín Prieto and his nephew General Manuel Bulnes, ruled the country during the first twenty years of the Conservative Republic) and the landowning aristocracy, who appeared to have exhausted their political energies in the factional and family rivalries of the first years of the revolution and who were increasingly satisfied with the role of passive supporters of the Conservative regime, which suited them admirably.

This political stability was naturally less secure than it appears in retrospect. Portales, its founder, considered it constantly jeopardized and felt that it required ceaseless vigilance. In fact, Conservative Chile was to be more celebrated for its capacity to weather storms than to avoid them. Even so, particularly after the victory over the Peruvian-Bolivian Confederation in the first Pacific War of 1837–1839, when the strength of Independent Chile was revealed, this country, risen from the most remote and isolated corner of the Spanish empire, came to enjoy unrivaled political prestige among the Spanish American republics.

At that juncture perhaps no country in Spanish America enjoyed less prestige than the Argentine Republic. By 1845 the crimes to be expected of the "tyrannic government" of the "fierce despot" who "made humanity groan" and "had already cut the throats of the most illustrious citizens of the Argentine provinces" had alarmed José Manuel Restrepo in his distant corner in Nueva Granada to the point of momentarily distracting him from things closer to hand.[14] The feeling that Argentina, under the aegis of Juan Manuel de Rosas, had descended to a level of political barbarity unknown in the rest of the continent was accepted throughout Spanish America. Nevertheless, the political solutions imposed by Rosas on Argentina and those imposed by far more prestigious conservative regimes on Nueva Granada and Chile had some elements in common, particularly with regard to their attitude toward the regular army.

In contrast to Chile and Nueva Granada, and like Venezuela, Argentina enlarged its military establishment during the wars of independence, which endowed the country with a large officer corps unwilling to accept economic hardship or political procrastination. The dissolution of centralized power in 1820 left this heritage to the new province of Buenos Aires, which took immediate action. One of the most celebrated reforms of its government during 1821–1824 pensioned off the greater part of the officers and arranged to use the remainder of the army to defend the Indian frontier, but after 1824 the war against Brazil brought the veterans out of retirement, and finding that the peace negotiated by the Federal party was unsatisfactory, they tried to take over the local government.

It was precisely against them and their systematic plundering that the countryside rose in arms in 1829 in a federalist revolution, the most talented leader of which was Juan Manuel de Rosas. Rosas never tired of describing the Federal victory as the result of the people's resistance to military despotism. In 1829 and again in 1835 he thoroughly purged the officer corps. The return of civil war, however (in which Rosas was well aware that his trump card was his control of Argentina's most powerful military organization), coupled with a succession of international wars, prevented him from permanently reducing the size of the army. Even so, his political strength was sufficiently independent of it to enable him, throughout the fifteen years in which he continuously used it, and in spite of constant currency inflation, never to increase the nominal pay of officers or men.

The sources of Rosas's political power were different from those

14 *Ibid.,* p. 442.

of the Conservative regimes in Chile or Nueva Granada. The rural militia on which he relied heavily in the early stages of his career was later systematically subordinated to the army and its powers limited, particularly after 1839, when it became apparent that it was a source of discord from which the officers of the Rosista army remained prudently aloof (being overwhelmed as they were not only by the close political supervision exercised by the government but by public opinion, which was more influential in Buenos Aires than in the rest of Spanish America after 1810 and which had swung in favor of the Federal party during the twenties). In the remaining Argentine provinces (excepting Córdoba, where an official of the National army assumed local power in 1820 and imposed upon the entire province the obligation of maintaining the armed forces under his command) the army originated in the militia and the Indian frontier defense force, and even in Córdoba it was gradually reduced in numbers and increasingly employed against the Indians. Here too the relative diminution of the army was accompanied by a parallel expansion of the militia.

The increased importance of the militia added to the political power of its leaders, a process considerably hastened when the latter were also important figures in provincial society (it was only when Rosas placed all the Argentine provinces under the hegemony of Buenos Aires that local governments began to be headed by militia leaders whose relative isolation with regard to locally dominant groups made them particularly receptive to orders from Buenos Aires). At the same time the emergence of a strong militia radically altered the internal structure of the provincial upper classes. Upper-class figures influential in those outlying areas with the most bellicose militias now became dominant and, not surprisingly were considered by the provincial capitals and far-off Buenos Aires to be as barbaric and as plebeian as the men they led.

With regard to this particular subject an exceptional witness of that turbulent period in Argentine history, General José María Paz, remarked that to maintain a political establishment the only alternative to the regular army was the gaucho.[15] But didn't the

---

[15] J. M. Paz, *Memorias postumas,* II (Buenos Aires, 1948): 122.

extreme dispersion of the military centers and the tensions which developed (in Argentina more than elsewhere) between the regular army, whose very survival was menaced, and the regional military groups and militias reflect the tension and oppositions characteristic of the entire new country in which, after the breakdown of the central state in 1820, a galaxy of provinces was condemned to dire financial straits while Buenos Aires became the almost exclusive heir to the country's fiscal revenue?

The peculiarities of militarization in different parts of Spanish America were frequently inherited from the remote past or due to local vicissitudes during the wars of independence and the varying effects of the new commercial freedom. All these factors account for the characteristics of militarization in the Andean countries of South America—Peru, Alto Peru (subsequently renamed Bolivia), and Quito, which attained its independence in 1830 as Ecuador. The slow and very partial character of postrevolutionary economic transformations imposed the main burden of supporting the state on the most isolated areas—the Ecuadorian and Peruvian Sierra and the Bolivian highlands. These same areas supplied the army with recruits in the shape of the Indians who had no influential protectors and who made up the greater part of the rank and file. The consequent displacement in the human and economic sources of military power was accentuated (and somewhat modified) by the vicissitudes characteristic of the wars of independence in the South American Andes.

The colonial presidency of Quito became first the Southern Department of Greater Colombia and in 1830 the Republic of Ecuador, whose first president was General Juan José Flores of Venezuela, supported by regular troops who were for the most part Venezuelan and whose skin appeared scandalously dark in a country in which the upper classes proudly flaunted blue eyes and fair hair. It would be wrong to assume that military power could be concentrated for long in the hands of the "black devils" from Venezuela. Very soon recurrent civil war made it necessary to increase the size of the army, using local recruits. As in Nueva Granada, in Ecuador the civil war mobilized for brief spans forces several times as large as the regular army. In 1833–1835 the aristocracy of Quito headed an unsuccessful rebellion against Flores, recruiting their men from the Sierra population. Ten years later the aristocracy of Guayaquil, who were more successful, mobilized their plebeian followers against the "Venezuelan Ethiopes," the "Caribs" of the Atlantic. Again, as in Nueva Granada, these vast mobilizations did not affect the economic and social predominance of the very traditional aristocracy which had launched them in order to wrest all power from its Liberators of 1822. Only gradually, as it became nationalized, did the army become an irreproachably vernacular rival to the local oligarchies, and even then it did not pose a permanent threat to aristocratic hegemony.

Why wasn't the dominance of the very traditional upper class destroyed during the course of a period of disorder which, by increasing the army's influence, appeared to make of it an alternative basis for political power? A partial explanation is afforded by the dominant influence of the Sierra, in which not only was the greater part of the population crowded, but the capital (which contained the highest proportion of whites) was also situated. The absence of any rapid expansion in the export economy of the coastal areas after 1810 was comparatively beneficial to the ruling class in the capital and to a lesser extent in some of the smaller highland towns, who were able to live in style off their lands. Their readiness (and that of the coastal aristocracy) to encourage uprisings by improvised groups outside the regular army reveals how little they had to fear from enlarging the armed forces with recruits from the lower levels of a society still scarcely aware of the possibilities of overthrowing the traditionally dominant sectors.

The situation was different again in Peru and Bolivia, which had been the most reliable strongholds of the royalist cause. True, from 1814 on there had been rebellions in southern Peru and Bolivia which had partly followed the traditional pattern of the Indian uprisings against the Spanish Crown. Here, however, the decisive factor was the recruitment of a predominantly indigenous population by the royalist army. This mobilization, firmly set in the mold of the regular army itself, left very little room for spontaneity on the part of the draftees, whose loyalty was in any case open to doubt from the start. When it became necessary to increase the number of officers, men of Creole origin and frequently of mixed blood, from families in many cases alien to any military tradition, were called upon. These leaders and soldiers were to form the basis of the new armies of the independent nations which only won their independence thanks to outside intervention from the north and south. After 1820 (i.e., after the revolutionary cause began to be successful) desertion increased among the royalist forces, and consequently, many ambitious scions of not too illustrious families who had started out serving the royalist flag reached the heights of their careers under that of the Republic. After the dissolution of Bolívar's Colombia (whose army replaced the Chilean-Argentinian followers of San Martín), the foreign element disappeared from the Peruvian balance of military power, and the National army—heir in many ways to that organized by the viceroys to fight revolution—became the indisputably dominant element in it.

More than one aspect of Peruvian militarization is reminiscent of the Mexican, with differences imposed by the environment. In Peru the export economy crisis in the coastal area and the reliance on the Indian levy, collected on a regional basis, as a source of revenue stimulated a tendency toward the regionalization of military and political power which only the advent of the guano export boom was to halt. Cuzco and to a greater extent Arequipa, which became revolutionary centers, were simultaneously the local ruling center and the military bases for the conquest of National power; it was no coincidence that the former should have been situated in the center and the latter on the borders of that massively Indian-populated sierra which had been the last royalist stronghold. The army leaders who endeavored to control these regional areas, and who frequently attempted to take over the whole country, did not necessarily represent any local higher group (although occasionally individual members of the local elites did take a part in their political adventures, to the disgust of their peers). Under these conditions the relationship of the socially and economically dominant sectors to the army leaders should be regarded, rather than as an alliance, as a state of reciprocal resignation which became increasingly inevitable because the local upper classes and the central government were unable properly to control the men and resources available to the military leaders and were thus not in a position to dispute the ascendancy of the latter. What remained to be seen was whether spontaneous affinity would make some of those leaders the supporters, rather than the rivals, of an elite whose ascendancy was of far longer standing than that of the military, who owed it to the recent wars. The expectation of a leader capable of imposing first upon the army, and then on the entire country, a political pattern which would satisfy the ambitions of that elite took a long time to die. Lamar, at times, Salaverry, and above all, Vivanco, successively personified this hope, but all of them failed in their bid for power. Their more fortunate rivals, Santa Cruz, whose ambitions transcended mere personal interest, the devious Gamarra, Lafuente, who for an unexpectedly long time was content to take second place, and even Castilla, who was finally able to impose political stability on the country thanks to the guano prosperity, were all, for different reasons, regarded with displeasure by the elite whom they in turn distrusted.

The fact that the officers of the Peruvian army appeared to be more professional than in other Latin American countries was less a result of their greater technical competence than that they had grown up within the structure of a regular military organization and that recruitment did not adhere strictly to the patterns of Peruvian society. The army owed its cohesion to the discipline imposed on the resigned Indian recruits, and its upkeep was assured by the Indian levy collected in the very areas controlled by its most powerful leaders. Compared to the regular army, a government-organized militia, or more spontaneous mobilizations, could achieve only secondary importance. While recruitment certainly increased in times of stress, it remained substantially the responsibility of the leaders of the regular army itself. Only in the coastal area the *montoneras* (or irregular forces), who did not rival it, were at least independent of the established military order. Their comparative weakness, however, and their irritating propensity for banditry made the traditional elite hesitate to support them, while an accumulation of very bitter experiences made it increasingly cautious in opposing the army whose hegemony effortlessly survived the downfall of the rulers it successively brought to power.

For somewhat similar reasons the regular army was equally dominant in Bolivia. Here foreign military influence disappeared late; that of the Peruvians, for instance, waned only in 1841, after their defeat at the battle of Ingaví. Even the officers of the Bolivian army frequently came from other Spanish American countries. Perhaps even more important was that the crisis of the colonial economy of Alto Peru centered in the silver mines, affecting the traditional urban centers and the upper sectors of society with which those centers were identified. Chuquisaca (city of enlightenment and aristocrats, administrative and judicial center of colonial Alto Peru, and capital of the country until the middle of the century, under the name of Sucre) suffered from the new economic adversity as much as Potosí, the great colonial mining center. A slow process of adaptation took place, but it took a long time for the newly emerging centers to become as influential as the old. In this temporary vacuum, created during the painful and lengthy transition from a colonial to a modern economy, the army found its opportunity, and it is hardly surprising that its dominant role should have been even less disputed than in Lower Peru, or that it should have found there more willing supporters among the educated classes who were aware of their weakness.

Militarization, subject to strong regional modifications, did not disappear with the end of the wars of independence, but its political consequences varied in different countries. Some, as in the case of Nueva Granada and for some time of several provinces of Argentina, were incapable of overcoming internal strife. Others had organized a solid political system which seemed not only to obviate this risk but to ensure the regular army a comparatively high degree of technical efficiency; this was *par excellence* the case in Chile and also in Argentina during the peak of the Rosista period. Finally, in yet others such as Mexico or Peru, the army dominated the political scene. What remain to be examined are the consequences of militarization with reference to the distribution of political power among social groups and to the concrete policies of governments where military influence was felt to a greater or lesser extent.

Undoubtedly, as Jorge Basadre has pointed out in the case of Peru, a military career in that disturbed period allowed more than one man, whose social origins in any other context would have denied him any political influence, to attain supreme command. Nevertheless, the magnitude of the possibilities of social improvement opened up by militarization must not be exaggerated. In some Spanish American countries, such as Nueva Granada, the traditional upper class retained its position in the officer corps, while in others, such as Chile and the provinces of Argentina, the officers of the regular army came either from among the more marginal members of the elite or from families which, since the days of the colony, had effortlessly controlled the military hierarchies. In others military power, be it that of the regular army or of the militias, lay indisputably in the hands of the most prominent members of society in subregions which had suddenly become important with the advent of war. This was the case of some of the Río de la Plata and Venezuelan caudillos.

Obviously, then, the chances of social improvement opened up by militarization were limited. Its relevance with regard to the policies adopted by the governments of the new countries is even more debatable. Until the middle of the nineteenth century the unanimously accepted social objective of the new politicians was to establish a solid order. In order to provide stability this order had to conform fairly closely to what survived of a prerevolutionary pattern which was difficult to replace. Perhaps no one better understood this necessity than some of the very people who had benefited from revolution and war. Páez is undoubtedly the best, but not the only, example of a caudillo of plebeian origin who devoted himself to consolidating an unmistakably conservative regime.

While altering the social structure was not among the direct objectives of any politically significant party, some political options had significant economic and social consequences. After the wars of independence had drained too many private individuals of their wealth, the universally shared objective appeared to become the reduction of public expenditure. However, although few denied this objective explicitly, such action as was taken by the governments of the new countries showed them not always overzealous in fulfilling it. There were individuals who preferred the rapid benefits derived from civil war to internal peace, accompanied by a depolitization process capable of slowly redirecting the energies of the emergent nations toward prosperity. Ambitious army men, members of the political class whom revolution had made preeminent in the government and who could not bring themselves to step down, and a multitude of unemployed lawyers were among those who kept the nostalgia of revolutionary struggles alive, together with the plebeians whom Restrepo reproached for their unheard-of desire to eat meat, which they could satisfy only as long as war made plunder permissible. All that sector of the population which was not to receive its share of the new wealth, the conquest of which was held by many to be the only legitimate goal of the new Spanish American states, could be classified among the potential supporters of civil war.

Not surprisingly, these same dissatisfied groups were bound to want a more complex and costly political and administrative apparatus regardless of the fact that it might not be the most efficient; also in this context the existence of a large military apparatus, frequently the deciding factor in the balance of political power, was crucial. The part which it played did not necessarily depend upon the social origins of its leaders, and it is interesting to compare the plebeian Páez, concerned with peace, security, and cheap and efficient administration, with the lordly Mosquera, who "is described as a spender, particularly insofar as the army is concerned."[16]

The officers did not everywhere side with the groups who preferred consumption to austerity and political to economic objectives. Even an army like the Mexican, which openly dominated the political scene and made use of the fact to appropriate an exorbitant part of the state revenue, eventually became associated with

16 Restrepo, *Diario,* May 30, 1846, III: 465.

the more conservative sectors, who resigned themselves to the onus of supporting it in spite of the fact that the alliance signified perpetual penury to the Mexican state. This in itself goes to show that the alternative courses were even more unsatisfactory to the propertied classes, and that the role of the army within the new social structure was as ambiguous as its position therein. While more than one officer, benefiting from the relaxation of social barriers which had accompanied the revolution, had risen from the ranks, the officer corps was expected to act as a barrier against the new equalitarian upsurge which the majority of the postrevolutionary leaders erroneously but almost unanimously regarded as an imminent threat.

Militarization, which was an essential part of the postrevolutionary scene, thus reflected the complexity, tensions, and contradictions which characterized the period itself. It would have been no easy task for the army at any time to defend an order whose leadership was fragmented, in which certain sectors or institutions lived on past prestige rather than present power and others had acquired more power than they realized. It was an even more difficult task because the army all too clearly reflected in its own vacillations and contradictions the blurred outline of this undeveloped order, principally characterized by its frailty. More than one observer blamed this frailty on the army itself, which, while ostensibly defending it, frequently helped to disrupt it. Although severely condemned by more considerate observers, many both within the armed forces and without found in civil war a temptation rather than a threat, even if it implied the unleashed destruction of crop and cattle and the enforced recruitment of the very countrymen whose toil had formerly ensured the prosperity of the propertied classes (who, moreover, were now offered the opportunity to plunder to counteract their tendency to desert), the despoliation of all the rich by army leaders in some areas, of only the hostile rich by the dominant warlords in areas where not only the army but the whole of society was split asunder by rival factions, and by all when chance arose.

Thus, in Arequipa, Peru, Flora Tristán could mockingly watch while her wealthy and avaricious relatives the Tristáns and Goyeneches sadly paid their tribute to the revolutionary who momentarily dominated the city. In San Juan de Cuyo, in the provinces of Argentina, a far poorer man, Domingo Sarmiento, had to buy his life for 2,000 pesos in silver from one of his own kinsmen, Facundo Quiroga, the successful leader of a rival political faction. All over Spanish America similar episodes were taking place, each faction throwing a veil over its own misdeeds but carefully recording those of its enemies.

While all this was enough to cause property owners unanimously to express their loathing of civil war, they had also far deeper and more serious criticisms to make. In their eyes the Spanish American order was too frail to survive repeated wars: they feared that political clashes would lead to open class warfare. It has already been seen how Restrepo avidly collected premonitory warnings of this in his chronicles of the Nueva Granada revolutions of 1839–1841. Bolívar, in stating that caste would fight against caste in a "colored war" which would open the abyss prepared by those who would not accept his increasingly conservative doctrines, was only the most prestigious of the leaders to use this argument, whose very frequency reveals how convincing it seemed. Much of its efficacy was due to the vivid recollection of the upheavals which accompanied the revolution (in the case of Bolívar, it seems at times as if, in prophesying a future of destructive war, he was merely foretelling a repetition of past struggles in which he himself took part and which in retrospect he may have found too brutal).

Among the frightened spectators of the time, the feeling that the future would probably be even more alarming than the past was based not only in their own personal experience, but in the lessons from outside events. Haiti, where a successful black uprising wiped out the entire European population, became an obsession in spite of the profound difference, which would have been obvious to more serene observers, between the structure of society in Saint-Domingue, made up of plantations supporting an exiguous white population, and countries in which the blacks were a minority. Nevertheless, these arguments do not entirely account for the constant foreboding of war between those who had and those who had not, even in societies in which caste differences were negligible. It is now hard to find solid objective bases for that blind pessimism in the postrevolutionary scene, and there are even signs that it was not always meant to be taken literally. It is remarkable, for instance, that while the subject of political Africanization remained fashionable, opposing factions were arming black troops wherever possible, from Peru and Venezuela to the Río de la Plata, where an inspired anti-Rosista poet, Juan Cruz Varela, reproached Rosas for using "African bands of vile slaves" as his supporters at the precise time when in the city of Montevideo in which Varela had taken refuge, the author of the Uruguayan national anthem, Francisco Acuña de Figueroa, was composing political songs for the black troops who were to fight against Rosas.[17]

Similarly, in spite of concern over the black threat both in Venezuela, where Bolívar was sure the African hordes would eventually prevail, and in Peru, where black outlaw bands on the very outskirts of Lima appeared to presage even more serious disturbances of the peace, slavery remained a fact. Flora Tristán, visiting the house and *ingenio* (sugar mill) of that refined aristocrat and model landowner and industrialist, Lavalle, close to the city of Lima, not only heard from him that the whip was a necessary stimulus for his 900 seminude slaves but also saw for herself entirely nude slave women imprisoned for allowing their children to starve to death. Lavalle was unafraid of living among his miserable slaves in a "little manufacturer's palace" decorated with English carpets, French furniture, clocks, and candelabra. In Venezuela an episode involving José Rafael Revenga, a former collaborator of Bolívar's, and the short-term president and forlorn hope of Venezuela's constitutionalists, Dr. José Maria Vargas, is even more significant. The slave of a man named Cuervo stole some goods from the *finca* (country estate) of Revenga in western Venezuela and was consequently handed over to the latter for punishment. Revenga beat the slave to death with his own hand, and Cuervo opened criminal proceedings against Revenga, who

[17] The text in J. L. Lanuza, *Cancionero del tiempo de Rosas* (Buenos Aires, 1941), p. 92.

sought and obtained the advice and sympathy of his friend Vargas. Vargas objected to the unjust persecution of Revenga; to denounce such justifiable conduct as his was a sign, he felt, of blind malevolence. What is particularly noticeable in this episode is that while correspondence on the case repeatedly cites the underhand action of old political enemies and the more open opposition of neighboring landowners who disliked Revenga (at times they seem to be reproached for taking the robberies to which Revenga was subjected too lightly), and while reference is made to the dangers of a sentimental reaction on the part of uninformed public opinion in Caracas to such drastic punishment for a petty crime, no mention is made of the possibility of any reaction whatsoever from the black population. Their passivity was taken entirely for granted by all three correspondents and implicitly also by Cuervo, who—in demanding five years' exile for his fellow landowner—was not by any means seeking to undermine the ascendancy of slave owners over their servants.[18]

Under circumstances such as these it is difficult to accept in its literal value the political and journalistic style of the period and its preference for prophecies of doom. But even admitting that in forecasting an apocalypse of social warfare the prophets of the time were not saying precisely what they intended, it is certain that in their deliberately alarmist language they were trying to convey a message. They probably based their misgivings on two different causes for concern with regard to the social stability of independent Spanish America. One originated in the very widespread realization of the intrinsic contradiction created in societies which, while professing to support equality, jealously preserved a state of social inequality and whose efforts at change never significantly contributed to bringing about the equalitarian ideal; but this realization only brought with it recognition of the need for eliminating the ideological validity of the equalitarian principle. The other cause for alarm derived from the belief that in postrevolutionary Spanish America war had destroyed essential components of the old, rigidly established structure and that the atrociously mutilated

18 J. M. Vargas, *Obras completas,* I (Caracas, 1958): 90–135.

surviving portion was no longer viable. Thus the prophets of class warfare who imagined all sorts of ferocious assaults upon the established order were perhaps only expressing the fear that it would collapse spontaneously even if confronted by quite weak challenges.

In this context it is easier to understand the fear of a black uprising. Revolution had affected slavery as an institution, and the changing attitude of the times rendered the importation of new slaves from Africa, essential because of their low birth rate in Spanish America, first unexpectedly costly and subsequently impossible. The continuance of slavery, or the return to this status of the Negro soldier who had been among the most efficient of the revolutionary recruits, became hazardous as well as contradictory to the general lines adopted by the postrevolutionary order. This cruelly absurd situation was explicitly remarked upon by foreign observers. When Basil Hall saw the slaves in the main square of Panama singing "not without taste and spirit a patriotic song of the day, originally composed in Buenos Ayres," he felt only compassion for those "poor people singing in praise of that liberty acquired by their masters from whose thought certainly nothing was further removed than the idea of extending the same boon to their slaves."[19] But while those directly affected preferred not to make their perplexity too evident, they became afraid that eventually slaves would not be willing to remain slaves in countries formally dedicated to the achievement of liberty and equality; it is therefore hardly surprising that fear should have begun to dominate not only the image of the future but also recollections of the past. Thus, whereas Hall, who was in Lima during the feverish period immediately preceding its liberation by the soldiers of San Martín, noted that "we sometimes fancied that the slaves were more cheerful than usual during this period" but hastened to add that such an impression was probably false and due to "our contrasting their undisturbed gaiety, for they were quite careless about the matter, with the doubt and gloom which beset every other

[19] B. Hall, *Extracts from a Journal,* II (Edinburgh, 1824): 124.

mind,"[20] Alexander Caldcleugh, who visited Lima only after its liberation, associated the Negroes not with mere suspicious cheerfulness but with "revolting disorders" of which their owners were among the first victims.[21]

That the relationship between slavery as an institution and the presumed danger from the Negroes was not inadvertent becomes apparent in the commentaries of José Manuel Restrepo with regard to the black disturbances in southern New Granada. After deploring the fact that General Obando, in search of support for his military plans, "had raised the sinister cry of freedom for slaves" and pointing out the role of agitators assumed by the former slaves whom the law of 1821 had freed, Restrepo concludes somewhat unexpectedly that although "the cry of freedom is alarming and we will still have to undergo several Negro disturbances . . . it is consoling [to know] that slavery is rapidly diminishing in consequence of the law of manumission previously referred to."[22] The risk of an uprising among the slaves, Restrepo logically concluded, would disappear with the abolition of slavery.

But the danger of subverting the racial hierarchy which, except in southernmost Spanish America, was the basis of social stratification did not depend only upon the risks inherent in maintaining slavery in countries formally dedicated to freedom. In spite of the fact that the Indian population far outnumbered the black and that it had played an active part in the past wars (with terrifying spontaneity in Mexico, or in passive obedience to those who had armed them, in the Andean countries), it was not regarded as so urgent a cause for concern once the revolutionary crisis was over. This was partly because their humble social status was not associated with such obviously objectionable institutions as slavery; and while even if their peculiar legal position was not altogether eliminated from all the new states, this was due to financial pressure rather than to a desire to defend social equilibrium. This, as has been mentioned earlier, was the case with the maintenance

---

[20] *Ibid.,* I: 193.
[21] A. Caldcleugh, *Travels in South America,* II (London, 1825): 68.
[22] Restrepo, *Diario,* May 14, 1843, III: 346.

of the Indian tribute as a source of revenue in Peru and Bolivia; moreover, the maintenance of this levy had its positive aspect insofar as it provided the new states with an incentive to defend Indian land statutes. The main reason why the Indian threat did not assume major proportions was, however, that the Indian continued to be regarded and to regard himself as a member of a nation parallel to the Spanish-Creole one—and hence not irrevocably integrated in it. This very distance between Indian and Creole was a significant factor in lessening tension. The Negro, on the other hand, was an integral part of the community in the most prosperous and dynamic areas of colonial economy and society (indeed only those sectors could afford the vast advance payment on labor costs which the acquisition of slaves implied). Moreover, for complex reasons which must be dwelt upon later, the pressure exerted by Spaniard and Creole upon the Indian was relatively small until the middle of the century and thus offered little incentive for an Indian uprising.

Mexico was an exception to this relatively tranquil Indian scene. In the forties the intensification of the wars in the north against the unsubdued Indians and the uprising of the Mayas in the Yucatán awoke fresh fears, recalling all too clearly the Indian multitudes which had followed Hidalgo and Morelos. It was at this juncture that José María Luis Mora stated that the first objective of Mexico after ending the war with the United States must be to subdue the colored population.[23] Even here, however, those memories and fears were insufficient to dissuade the different political factions from using Indian support whenever available. As François Chevalier noted, once the Mexican Indians had associated the liberals with the reform laws which threatened their territorial heritage, it was mainly the Conservatives who were able to gain their support.[24] Their opportunistic reasons for seeking Indian support are easily discernible, but it remains significant that they could have

[23] J. M. L. Mora to Luis de la Rosa, May 31, 1848, Hale, *Mexican Liberalism*, p. 241.

[24] François Chevalier, "Conservateurs et libéraux au Mexique: Essai de sociologie et géographie politiques de l'indépendance a l'intervention française," in *Cahiers d'Histoire Mondiale*, III, 3 (Paris, 1964), 461–463.

made use of it, even by arming Indians for civil war, without forfeiting their identity as the party of order and stability in the eyes of their Creole adherents in the capital and most of the larger cities.

Since the distance between Spaniard and Creole on the one side and the Indian population on the other eliminated an immediate Indian threat, the very existence of the Indians could be deliberately ignored. In Mexico, according to Mora, there were no more Indians since their peculiar legal status had been eliminated. But since they were daily to be seen where they always had been, they were referred to as the "so-called Indians" by a simultaneous process of recognition and rejection.[25] In this instance the gap between unchanging reality and the revolutionary ideals, far from being a cause of tension, as in the case of the black versus the white population, appears to have been regarded as an added insurance against the possibility of caste warfare. The danger of future apocalyptic strife appeared less justified in the case of the Indian and never became a generalized cause for concern, even in a postrevolutionary Spanish America, always prone to eye the future pessimistically.

The equilibrium of the colonial caste system thus appears to have been less affected by the revolution, and above all by newer and more radical changes, than many contemporary observers would have admitted. Nevertheless, that equilibrium was faced not only with the threat of a head-on collision between the most and the least privileged castes of pre-1810 society, but by other, more insidious threats with which it was less able to cope.

While Bolívar horrified his audience by predicting a future in which the country would be ruled by the black population, he was distressed by alarming signs in the present. In traveling through Ecuador he found the brown-skinned groups, to whom he referred as the *pardocracia* (as opposed to the *albocracia,* or white aristocracy), to be prevailing.[26] Who were those dusky aristocrats whom

---

[25] Hale, *Mexican Liberalism,* p. 128.
[26] Bolívar to Santander, Ibarra, October 8, 1826, Bolívar, *Obras completas,* II (Havana, 1947): 1441.

Bolívar contrasts to the white who had preserved southern Colombia's inherited order as "an absolute dogma" with the tacit assent of the Indians and nowhere better than in Popayán, "the beloved province, fatherland of Arboleda and Mosquera"?[27] In speaking of the *pardocracia* Bolívar was referring to men whom colonial rule had denied the key positions, but who were sufficiently well educated to abuse the freedom of the press. They were the descendants of the same dusky-skinned people to whom, in 1795, the Spanish Crown had been prepared to sell titles—to the indignation of the aristocracy of Caracas, who were loath to admit dark-skinned parvenus in their ranks. If Popayán appeared admirable to Bolívar it was because "magistrates, leaders and honorable population" were grouped as in prerevolutionary times around "the Mosqueras, Arroyos and their families" and because the venerable leader of that hierarchy which had managed to ride the revolutionary storm was also the head of the most powerful local dynasty, Joaquín Mosquera, the "virtuous patriarch of Popayán."[28]

The fact that the rest of Colombia so little resembled Popayán was due precisely to the revolution, not only because it unwittingly prepared the ground for the clashes of huge forces out to defend their inflamed caste loyalties but because it set out deliberately to attack the small group of European-born Spaniards who occupied the foremost administrative and commercial positions and who made up the nucleus of the prerevolutionary elite. Once victory had been achieved, the size of the politically influential groups inevitably increased, and before long the movement which had originally comprised a sector of the prerevolutionary elite spread to lower levels of society. At this juncture, its promoters began to find that democratization had already gone too far.

Among the ruling sector which revolution had both decapitated and swollen, the notion that caste barriers had been irrevocably torn down eventually became accepted. Its new members sustained that caste differences, the basis of the hierarchical organization they wished to destroy, had always been meaningless. This declaration was dangerously easy to prove owing to the fact that after

---

[27] Bolívar to J. R. Arboleda, Canbal, October 11, 1826, *ibid.,* II: 1443.
[28] Bolívar to T. C. de Mosquera, Bogotá, November 15, 1828, *ibid.,* II: 505.

the Conquest caste separation only gradually became rigid. Thus many families legally considered Spanish were in reality of mixed origins (at the time of the Spanish Conquest, a mixture of Spanish and princely Indian blood had not been regarded as a disgrace but rather as honorable proof of the early establishment of the bearer's family in the Indies). In a society predisposed to fear its own tolerance of new-made men, there was an ever-increasing and malevolent preoccupation over heredity. In many cases the new notables, whose success was supposedly due to revolutionary condemnation of caste differences, belonged by right since colonial times to the very elite which spurned their "impure" origins. Thus, in the Argentine provinces in the thirties, the governor of Tucumán was referred to as "el Indio Heredia" (Heredia the Indian), but was in fact the son of a prosperous member of the colonial urban elite, a colonel in the National army and a deputy to the National Constituent Congress in 1824. His rise to the post of governor may, however, have exasperated the susceptibilities of his peers toward his ethnic insufficiencies (he had, in fact, been a somewhat marginal figure in Tucumán politics and owed his good fortune entirely to his good standing with Facundo Quiroga, head of the province of La Rioja, who in 1832 conquered Tucumán for the Federal party). In neighboring Salta, on the other hand, reference was made only obliquely to the equally mixed origins of one of the most influential traditional families, since it would have been both unnecessary and discourteous to explain further the "uniformly copper" complexion of the Saravias.[29]

Together with that growing sensitivity toward the changes in the social equilibrium supposedly revealed by the presence of too many dark skins among the leaders of the new states, a more alert awareness of the strictly ethnic aspects of caste differentiation was also responsible for the increased attention paid to blood differences. This awareness was rendered more acute by the almost universal acceptance of an ideal racial type which was scarcely to be found in Spanish America. Thus, to explain the success achieved by a somewhat effeminate French viscount among the

[29] B. Frías, *Historia del general Güemes y de la provincia de Salta,* I (Salta, 1902): 227.

ladies of Arequipa, Flora Tristán could remark that "in Peru blue eyes and fair hair are the two signs of beauty which are most esteemed."[30] The relationship between the acceptance of the superiority of an unusual physical type and the growing prestige of the nations in which it was most usual is clearly perceptible in the memoirs of Mariquita Sánchez of Buenos Aires, who referred to the contrast between the local soldiers and the British invaders of the Río de la Plata in the following terms: "The militia of Buenos Aires: It must be confessed that our country folk are not good-looking. They are strong and robust, but black. Their heads are round, dirty. . . ." The invaders, on the other hand, not only wore "a most poetic uniform" but one which also set off their "most beautiful youthfulness and faces of snow" thanks to "the cleanliness of these admirable troops."[31] Dark skin was regarded as the legitimate companion of dirt, and snow-white faces the natural complement of cleanliness and elegance. It is, moreover, interesting to note the influence which the image of the racial balance in Spanish America conjured up by those privileged witnesses, the foreigners, had upon the image which Spanish American society was forming of itself. Already in colonial times the foreigner had discovered that Spanish America was far less Spanish than it considered itself to be.

Is this to say that the progress of the mixed castes was a sort of optical illusion on the part of the beholder? The answer must be complex and allow scope for local variations. It is true that in Venezuela caste equilibrium was seriously affected by the revolution, which here more than anywhere else was responsible for the emergence of leaders of very humble social origins. Similarly, in Mexico, where the greater part of the revolutionary leaders were members of the predominantly Creole provincial elite, Guerrero, for instance, could be described by Bolívar as the "vile abortion of a savage Indian and a fierce African."[32] Insofar as caste equilibrium is concerned, the alteration of the interregional balance must

---

[30] F. Tristán, *Peregrinaciones* (Santiago de Chile, 1941), p. 32.

[31] M. Sánchez, *Recuerdos* (Buenos Aires, 1953), p. 66.

[32] Bolívar, *Obras,* II: 1300.

also be taken into account. The victory of the black population which Bolívar feared in Nueva Granada was identified for him with that of the coastal north, where even the elite had an admixture of black blood. In Peru the voluble reproaches directed by the aristocracy of Lima at Gamarra and his wife did not always distinguish between their Cuzqueño origins and the fact that they were mestizos (half-castes). Less dramatically, in Bolivia the decline of the colonial urban centers and the gradual increase in the importance of La Paz signified, among other things, the victory of the mestizo elite over the Spanish. All these instances merely add to the conclusions already reached when examining the influence of militarization of the social structure of Spanish America: although changes in the prerevolutionary equilibrium were far from absent, they were less frequent than is to be assumed from the disconsolate comments of the observers of the time, who were predisposed to condemn any social pattern which did not rigidly conform to prerevolutionary hierarchical differentiations between hereditary groups.

Páez, Flores, and Guerrero were exceptional. Furthermore, even the outstanding mestizo generals who occupied so prominent a place in the history of Peru, and the *pardos* of Venezuela, did not normally feel any compulsion to place their power at the service of caste solidarity, an emotion which they seemed to feel only intermittently. But although many of the parvenus were too engrossed in being accepted as rightful members of the surviving elite to remember their former peers (already in 1826 with Páez in mind, Bolívar was pointing out that those who had by that time acquired something they could lose were perfectly aware of "the dangers of siding with the mob"), those who were loyal to their followers, as were Guerrero and Juan Alvarez in Mexico, were repaid by their grateful support,[33] and even politicians of unimpeachable Spanish and Creole origin made use of these marginal groups whenever opportunity arose. Thus, in Caracas, Antonio Leocadio Guzmán, after paying assiduous court to Bolívar and Páez, to the British

[33] Bolívar to Santander, Pasto, October 14, 1826, *ibid.,* I: 1446.

merchants and the Creole elite, sought greater power by promoting a rebellion under the rallying cry of "death to the whites."[34]

Both the sincere political loyalty of Juan Alvarez and the pure opportunism of Guzmán prove that a political clientele existed which could be won by opposing traditional caste differences. A clientele or rather two: one was essentially rural and was primarily of military use to those who could win its support: from the south of Mexico to the north of Nueva Granada, the south of Chile and the Mission province in the Río de la Plata, leaders who sometimes raised the anachronistic banner of the Spanish king and in other cases that of the Federation, but who explicitly adopted the pose of revindicating the marginal mestizos or Indians, were able to create or to extend the bases of their military strength. The second sort was urban, and their utility more directly political. They were a complex group comprising people of whom little is known. The demagoguery of their speakers together with a sort of holy terror of the equalitarian principles characteristic of their adversaries conjures up a picture of the group which stresses the importance of the lowest strata of society, but members of this level were not predominant or by any means the exclusive component thereof. Together with the lowest of the populace, we find members of the urban elite (generational and family rivalries being intense enough, as will be seen subsequently, to justify the interruption of class loyalty in entire groups, while the labyrinthine quality of the personal conflicts which divided this sector is sufficient to explain the occasional defection even of veteran elite politicians). The greater part of the group comprised members of an intermediate sector of society, in the shape of the artisans who occupied a scarcely defined position in the colonial setup but who had found in it, and were to find in the new context created by Independence, opportunities to increase their wealth. In the 1840s it was they who, from Santiago de Chile to Bogotá, suddenly took up politics. In Buenos Aires, where Rosas sought to identify himself with them, they were known as the *gente de chaqueta* or jacketed people, as opposed to the proud *unitarios* who wore dress coats (it

[34] Restrepo, *Diario,* May 31, 1848, III: 558.

should be recalled in this context that the jacket was a relatively expensive piece of apparel and far from common among the poorer sectors of the population). While the Negro as such hardly figured among the artisans, partial black ancestry was by no means unusual among them, and their increasing political influence, due at least in part to their improved economic position, apparently entails, albeit in a partial and limited fashion, the collapse of the colonial caste system.

From the point of view of social equilibrium the increasing presence of members of the lower and marginal groups of urban society on the political scene was, however, less significant. In the first place, their presence followed the traditional pattern of availability for those acts of violence and pillage already feared by the old regime, rather than continuous support along established political lines. Second, they were urgently concerned with objectives other than a face-to-face political struggle against inequality. While the presence of the lower classes could no longer be ignored by the governments, it was still possible to avoid open conflict with them and even to use them as a political instrument without touching their social status in any essential way.

To sum up, the effect of Independence upon large groups of determinate caste, such as the Indians (who merely retained their marginal position and some of their own peculiar laws) or the Negroes of the mining and agricultural areas, was less marked than its effect on the equilibrium between the different castes—and social groups—in the cities, where the divisions between them were more imprecise and fluid and had been so since colonial times. The progressive blurring of caste barriers resulted not only from the moderate pressure exerted by the lower classes or from the limited possibilities for social progress afforded by the new regime. Far more important was the crisis among the urban elite, which reduced the distance between it and the intermediate urban groups. That very elite which caused the revolution had been affected by it more than any other sector of society. Its nucleus had been made up almost everywhere of Spaniards; only in Venezuela were the upper-class landowning Creoles more powerful and prestigious than the Spanish merchants and dignitaries; in Mexico the predominantly Creole ownership of the silver mines (in which, however, the Spanish also had a share) made the Creoles equal in wealth to the old Spaniards. In marginal areas, isolated from Spanish bureaucracy, while the importance of the Creole elite was also considerable, prior to the revolution they lacked that internal solidarity and that familiarity with the administrative apparatus which were the key to the power of the Spanish.

Now, the Spanish were the predestined victims of the revolution which sought from the outset to wrest control of the bureaucracy from them. The ambitions of the Creoles did not stop there, however. Gradually the corporations, the Church, and the religious orders became battlegrounds in which the revolutionary authorities were by no means impartial arbiters. Soon, abandoning hopes which were probably insincere from the start, the revolutionary authorities decided that all old Spaniards who could not prove otherwise would be regarded as enemies and treated accordingly. It was no fortuitous circumstance that those Spaniards who were not members of the elite, such as the Canary Island colonists of Venezuela, and small merchants all over Spanish America, should have met with particularly fierce persecution. But while members of the Spanish elite had less to fear than their more insignificant fellow countrymen, being somewhat better protected by their connections with the not always unfriendly Creole elite, even their position became increasingly difficult. They were subjected everywhere to precautionary measures which ran from deportation to lands more securely held by the revolutionary forces, to serious limitations on their personal freedom. Even in the relatively safe city of Buenos Aires they were forbidden to ride on horseback or to leave their houses at night, nor could they act as traders or executors. They were, moreover, forbidden to marry Creoles and forced to contribute to the support of the revolutionary forces. In fact, their impoverishment, particularly where they had not been quick enough in removing the wealth they had accumulated by trading, and where persecution started early, became a necessary consequence of this policy. In Buenos Aires, Santiago de Chile, and Lima, the Spaniards who had formerly occupied the foremost place in society now found it difficult to occupy any place at all, and the British and North American travelers of the time, who were able to watch the merciless liquidation of a whole sector of society by its closest enemies, and who did not always find the revolutionary harshness justifiable, could only pity and deplore their fate.

The most paradoxical aspect of this simultaneously hostile and intimate relationship, and also that richest in consequences, was the immediate replacement in key positions of the Spaniard by the Creole, a process which was the natural outcome of the takeover of one generation from another. Although it was suggested at one point that the stigma of Spanish nationality should be transmitted to the children of Spaniards born in the Indies, the very fact that the originator of this idea was himself the son of a Spaniard brought home the impossibility of applying such a solution. In fact, even the American descendants of Spanish families who were notorious for their open resistance to the revolutionary cause were frequently spared the consequences of their common heritage. In the Río de la Plata the children of the former mayor, Martín de Alzaga, who was executed in 1812 as a conspirator, not only inherited their father's wealth but were able to pursue their public careers under revolutionary governments, and the son of a high-ranking officer of the royalist army, and nephew of yet another, both of whom had left Buenos Aires after the revolution in disgust at the political situation, was able to pursue his career in the revolutionary forces, in spite of having started out serving the royalist cause, and eventually became a general.[35]

In spite of these mitigating circumstances, the Spanish as a whole suffered bitterly when political links with Spain were severed. Their removal from the highest stratum of colonial society gave their Creole rivals the choice of careers in commerce and the higher ranks of civil, military, and ecclesiastical administration, but in both these fields their expectations of rapid profits were doomed to disappointment. Commercially speaking, the causes were not so much related to the sociopolitical crisis induced by the

[35] Tulio Halperin-Donghi, "Revolutionary Militarization in Buenos Aires, 1806–1815," *Past and Present*, 40 (July 1968): 99.

revolution as to the economic changes resulting from closer association with more sophisticated economies than that of Spain, as will be seen subsequently, but the growing disillusion of the Creoles who obtained high administrative positions was the logical but unexpected consequence of the political requirements of the revolutionary governments.

The revolutionary governments were bound to be radically different in their objectives and tactics from the colonial administration which they superseded. That this difference was not only due to altered political ideals is proved by the fact that royalist strongholds underwent an analogous process. Under the Spanish power had been wielded by a distant authority whom long experience had taught to distrust to a greater or lesser extent all its local agents and to preserve that equilibrium between them which would best allow it to retain its own supremacy. The revolutionary governments, established on the spot, could not expect to cope so indirectly. By broadening their sphere of immediate action, they not only fulfilled one of their aims, but also what was perhaps an essential requirement for their survival. Following the revolution, during the struggle for independence which was substantially a civil war, rival powers had closely to control the entire administrative apparatus not only to prevent it from using its own initiative in ways that could be dangerous for the movement as a whole, but also to ensure its dubious loyalty. The reduction of the authority of the local magistrates who had been so powerful in colonial times was hence inevitable. It was equally inevitable that this process should have curtailed not only their powers of decision but also their very prestige. The revolutionary authorities were definitely aware of the additional difficulties which their own novelty created for them. They lacked that implicit recognition of their legitimacy which only habit and the passage of time would grant them from their subjects. It was for this excellent reason that, on purging the administrative apparatus of royalist sympathizers, the revolutionary governments also took steps to prevent the creation of revolutionary heirs for these dangerous foes in the shape of bureaucrats who might install themselves in some corner of the apparatus like feudal lords in their fortresses. Very understandably, the new and insecure revolutionary governments endeavored to avoid creating rivals for themselves.

The consequences of this basic attitude were further aggravated by the fundamental instability of the political process and the consequent instability of the servants whom the revolutionary governments employed. Already in colonial times the careers of government personnel which remained separate at lower levels were interrelated at higher levels: thus, a provincial governor or even a viceroy could have been promoted from the law courts, from the army, or even from the clergy. This characteristic was but the mildest foretaste of the capricious course the careers of the administrative employees were to follow under the revolutionary governments. Thus they were prevented from identifying themselves too closely with the different positions which they held throughout the course of their careers. In this way all public career eventually merged into that which a cynical witness of the revolution of the Río de la Plata, General Tomás Iriarte, called "the career of the revolution." But this career was rich above all in disappointments, and its followers became increasingly less prestigious. As the implicit risks involved became more apparent, those with something to lose refused to become involved in them, and this decision, born primarily of prudence, eventually acquired both social and moral justification. Public life was for those who had no other way of prospering, and it was thus hardly surprising that public service became a somewhat disreputable calling. Naturally, this conclusion was not always valid, but even the revolutionary leaders most closely associated with the ideal of orderly administration and respectful of private interest were too frequently called upon to sacrifice private interest to the interests of the state, and the victims of the aggressively impoverished revolutionary states were not always impartial enough to distinguish between the results of the situation in which the state found itself and the personal inclinations of its leaders.

Thus the revolutionary rulers, almost all of them members of the prerevolutionary Creole elite (except in places like Venezuela, where the revolution met with too many setbacks), became estranged from the elite, which considered them with growing mistrust.

Already prior to the revolution, the generous margin of corruption allowed by the administrative system caused high-ranking officials to be more frequently feared than respected. Subsequently, the instability of the new political situation and the repetitive pattern of the downfall of the momentarily powerful made even fear less effective. Furthermore, in a regime born of the stimulus of war, and which faced dangerous internal discord, the sectors of the bureaucracy who best kept an effective autonomy of decision were those most directly involved with the new aspects of administration created by this state of affairs, i.e., army officers, police, and local functionaries who carried out very complex tasks within a reduced geographical—and predominantly rural—area and whose attributes were considerable but not too clearly defined. In other words, effective power was no longer concentrated in those posts which had the greatest prestige in colonial times, and from which the Creole elite had sworn to remove the civil servants whom the Spanish Crown had recruited primarily from Spain.

The ecclesiastical positions which the revolution opened to the Creole elite suffered a parallel loss of prestige. There was no part of Spanish America in which ecclesiastical wealth did not suffer at the hands of the revolution. The abandoned convents from Mexico southward, which occasionally housed schools or libraries but which more frequently became army quarters or government offices, bore eloquent witness to this fact. To begin with, the churches and religious orders in country districts were spared, but eventually pressure of circumstance led to the takeover of lands, slaves, cattle, crops, and treasures. The liquidation of the Church's riches was supervised by the clergy, who, reluctantly or not, were obliged to turn to politics in order to survive. In royalist-held areas the Church raged against the revolution from the pulpit. The revolutionaries, using tactics which ranged from open intimidation to adulation, sought for their part to turn the clergy of the areas which they held into their political agents. The double crisis in the Spanish American church's relations with Rome and Madrid made for its more complete capitulation to local authority, and colonial tradition had taught the clergy, while not eluding conflict, to accept secular authority. The consequences of the politicization of the Church, that is to say, its acceptance of the fact that its material and spiritual power had to be placed at the service of a political cause, could only lead to the collaboration of the ecclesiastical authorities themselves in its impoverishment. This reduced the attraction of an ecclesiastical career, as reflected in the almost universal drop in the number of people entering the clergy after the declaration of independence.

For the Church and the magistrates the revolution signified a loss, rather than an increase in wealth and influence, and consequently an irreparable loss of prestige. The postrevolutionary process was unable to correct this situation. The financial problems of the new states, combined with the recognition given to the priority of military expenditure, made it impossible to return prosperity to the bureaucracy. On the other hand, however, the fact that the instability of the political situation almost nowhere affected the stability of postrevolutionary bureaucracy reveals how insignificant the bureaucracy had become.

Thus the Creole elite of the former Spanish colonies were unable to achieve, in the new order created by revolution, the eminent positions they had relied upon obtaining by helping to unleash the process. In the new political system in which naked force played a far more decisive part than it had formerly, power, and the advantages derived therefrom, were to be found where strength lay, and within the structure of the central state, strength lay in the hands of the army, of all institutions that least subject to control by the Creole prerevolutionary elite.

Frequently, however, the central state was not able to survive the increasing complexity and dispersion of its sources of power. New structures, competing with, or taking the place of, those which the revolution had hoped both to preserve and to place at the disposal of the new rulers, now found support outside the old centers of government. This dispersion of the sources of power, and of power itself, was partly a consequence of the course of the revolution (a course both more violent and less subject to control by certain sectors of the elite than had been surmised in 1810), but also a consequence of the economic changes which the revolution brought with it by opening up trade relations with the most developed economic centers of the day.

2

THE NEW COMMERCIAL ORDER

In 1839 Fanny Calderón was looking out the window of her lodgings on the houses of the main street of Veracruz. They were richer and more elegant than could have been expected in that inhospitable and insalubrious port, and a particularly fine and well-cared-for house drew her attention. "I find," she adds, "it belongs to an English merchant." Some days later, in the old town of Jalapa, which was little more than "a few very old steep streets with some large and excellent houses," she felt entitled to draw a general conclusion: "the best, as usual, belonging to English merchants."[1] Twenty years earlier, in Buenos Aires, the representative of the United States government observed that the English merchants had begun to buy the best houses and deduced from this that they were preparing to settle down for a long time. In Pocuro, a tiny Chilean town, an English butcher built himself a house "which appears palatial in these surroundings, greatly to the admiration of his neighbors."[2] In Islay, a village on the deserted Peruvian coast, which served as a port for Arequipa, the enchanting house of the English consul stood out against a background of miserable cane huts.[3] Flora Tristán remarked disapprovingly on the somewhat ostentatious luxury of the British merchants throughout Peru, and in Bogotá, when the exceedingly wealthy Arrubla sold his sumptuous house, it was once again an Englishman, the consul, who bought it.[4] These were but a few indications of the secure establishment of a new dominating group within the urban and mercantile economy.

---

[1] Frances Calderón de la Barca, *Life in Mexico* (London, n.d.), pp. 40, 50.
[2] M. Graham, *Diario* (Madrid, 1916), p. 187.
[3] F. Tristán, *Peregrinaciones* (Santiago de Chile, 1941), pp. 50, 109.
[4] J. Hamilton, *Travels,* I (London, 1827): 138.

There was no mystery involved in the establishment of British merchants of not very high social standing (María Graham found the social behavior of the English residents in Chile shockingly vulgar and attributed it to their comparatively humble origin) in the highest spheres of Spanish American society.[5] The liberalization of trade had made possible an influx of foreign merchant groups which the leading local merchants of the latter stages of the colonial period were particularly badly prepared to face. Their weakness was that of the Spanish economy itself. Insofar as the provision of European goods was concerned, their role was almost entirely that of middlemen. The revolution not only opened up the new Latin American markets to the world, but simultaneously closed the Spanish market which the Peninsular war between 1808 and 1813 and before then the war with the British had rendered almost inaccessible. Spanish America urgently needed to establish new commercial contacts to take the place of those which, even before the revolution, had become more distant. In this context the consequences of commercial liberalization were more immediate and far more devastating than they would have been if this process had taken place under less abnormal circumstances.

The opening up of trade to the British was the most important aspect of the new situation. The United States had been trading already with Spanish America during the years of progressive isolation from Spain which preceded the revolution. Trade with continental Europe became possible only after the peace of 1814, and it was some time before it could significantly penetrate the new markets. England, on the other hand, was ideally situated to dominate the Spanish American market. International politics played into her hands. Both reluctant Spain, now an ally, and the rebel colonies depended too much on British good will to refuse her the trading rights she desired. It was especially hard for the fragile revolutionary governments to prevent British commercial penetration, because at that juncture British support was considered essential to their very survival. This privileged position not only brought about the consolidation of a free-trade policy but also

[5] Graham, *Diario,* pp. 227, 295.

redounded to the benefit of the British merchants in other ways as
well. They were, for instance, better protected than their Creole
rivals from the financial exactions of hard-pressed revolutionary
governments. The need to preserve British favor was not, however,
the only restrictive influence on the economic initiatives of the new
states. Precisely because the revolutionary governments were unable to face any reduction in their revenues during the wars, when
their expenditures were soaring, they could not undertake reforms
of the tax system which might imperil, however briefly, an income
increasingly dependent on the volume of foreign trade. Thus, while
the economy as a whole might suffer from excessively rapid expansion of imports, the new Spanish American states did little to
prevent this expansion from taking place and indeed allowed the
liberalization of trade to reach its most extreme limits.

The predicament of the new Spanish American states was not
alone in favoring the British. After 1808, when the Portuguese
court moved to Rio de Janeiro, Brazil became an even more direct
economic dependency of Great Britain, and the privileged place of
the latter in the Brazilian economy has been recognized by treaty
since 1810. Rio de Janeiro became a center for distribution and
warehousing of British goods, and its location made it particularly
well suited as a base for commercial penetration into the southern
sector of the former Spanish empire.

The British were eager to make full use of these opportunities:
with the European market closed to them during an extremely
costly war, Britain was hardly likely to disdain a new market,
particularly, although not exclusively, for industrial goods. Rather
than make slow and prudent advances in these newly opened
Spanish American markets, the British flooded them with an
avalanche of not very carefully chosen exports. That they should
have adopted this strategy was due rather to a surplus of manufactured goods than, as Spanish American observers supposed, to a
deliberate policy of annihilating any possible competition on the
part of local traders. All too frequently this dangerous tactic took
its toll on the invaders themselves. There was the case—and it was
by no means exceptional—of those British merchants who, after
living splendidly in Santiago de Chile for a while, were subse-

quently forced to move to Valparaíso to eke out a precarious living selling small quantities of imported goods at a diminutive profit in a market unable any longer to absorb the flood of merchandise which those same merchants had been imprudent enough to initiate,[6] while the less fortunate among them had already been forced to abandon the scene of their ephemeral successes. But if the purpose of the British merchants was not that which was attributed to them by suspicious observers, the results of their activities were only too apparent: in dumping into these avid markets cheaper goods than had ever been seen before, with dizzying speed the British destroyed an entire commercial system.

One of the most destructive weapons in the British traders' arsenal was the introduction of ready cash in a trade network traditionally dominated by credit. Again, this was not a means of deliberate aggression but a consequence of the very fact that the first wave of British merchant penetration was oriented toward short-term speculation. The British were endeavoring not so much to establish permanent trading connections as to make the most of a market situation which might or might not last. They proceeded to carry out a rapid succession of transactions, after each of which profits were withdrawn hastily in the shape of money or goods, but preferably the former, as Britain was primarily interested in disposing of surplus manufactured goods. The traders started out by using money in their transactions. This device had several advantages: chiefly that it allowed them to negotiate directly with the producers and small traders in outlying districts who until that time had been hampered by debts which tied them to their larger creditors.

Even in most of the larger ports, the situation was similar. The systematic use of sales by public auction enabled the British traders to deal directly both with the consumer and with the small merchant, whose position—compared with that of the more important merchants—was no better than that of the producers and merchants of outlying country districts. It was primarily the cheapness of the commodities offered on a cash (or on a fixed, generally

[6] J. Miers, *Travels,* I (London, 1826): 447–448.

short-term credit basis) which appealed to the consumer and to the middleman, all of whom previously had been used to making extensive use of credit. The takeover of the market by the British from the Spanish was thus accelerated by a partial redistribution of wealth which favored producers and small merchants and enabled them to alter their manner of operation. One aspect of this new tendency is reflected in Chile. There appeared a number of small traders of Creole origin who found it easier to survive and even to prosper with the British than with the Spanish and who, according to Miers, comprised "a new and independent race of shopkeepers" who rose out of nowhere and had been able to take advantage of the fact that the British, anxious to unload their produce, had sold at a loss.[7] As Miers repeatedly observed, they were independent of the larger merchants (who had financed the small merchants in the past) but not of the landowning class, who, Miers was certain, were the source of their capital. This hypothesis (which he states as a fact) requires further study, but it is in any case true that the new market forces allowed the small traders to prosper on an unprecedented scale.

The advantages the new commercial system offered to producers were even more evident. Proof of this was the fact that local prices of export goods increased and, despite occasional dips, only under exceptional circumstances returned to prerevolutionary levels—of course it should be remembered that prerevolutionary price levels were depressed not only by local restrictions but also by the increasing obstacles which war placed in the way even of official trade. Here, again, the use of ready cash accelerated the transition. Cash itself was such an innovation that the Robertson brothers could boast of having introduced money to the province of Corrientes in eastern Argentina, where prior to their arrival even purchases for daily consumption were carried out by barter. Cash, together with the freedom of movement which their status as British subjects gave them, allowed the Robertsons to buy at rock-bottom prices the cattle which the ranchers preferred to sell at a loss rather than lose as war casualties. It was the availability of ready cash which channeled to the producers a larger share of the prosperity which the old system had restricted to the leading merchants. The liberating effect of the changeover from credit to cash, typical of this period of transition, was, however, short-lived: almost everywhere the consolidation of British mercantile ascendancy was followed by a return to the use of credit in trade.[8]

Whatever the intentions of the British, the result was indisputable. After 1820 merchants connected to the British economy occupied the dominant position held until 1810 by the emissaries of the traders (and, to a lesser extent, the producers) of the Spanish Peninsula. The fate of the copper miners of Copiapó, as related by Hall and corrected by Miers, summarizes the whole process. The miners, according to Captain Hall, had suffered under the merciless exploitation of their Spanish *habilitadores* or backers. A miner received from his *habilitador* the money necessary to work a claim, and until he had repaid his debt, he was obliged to sell to him the mineral extracted from the mine, at a fixed price below the market one. This not only afforded the backers a welcome additional source of income but also ensured that the miner would be unable to pay off his debt, since the profits allowed him by the contract sales price made this impossible. An English merchant saved the unfortunate miner from his drudgery by advancing him the money to pay his debt and allowing him to repay it at current rates of interest. The miner sold his produce to his new backer at market price and, stimulated by the prospect of greater profits, rapidly increased his production, thus in the long run benefiting his savior. According to Miers this edifying anecdote is unfortunately inaccurate. He claims that Hall received his information from some British merchants who, far from behaving like the savior in their story, had crushed both the miners and their former backers and held both to ransom, ensuring for themselves an exorbitant share in the profits. Miers takes no exception to their attitude and states that it was "the practice of their trade as mer-

---

[8] See Tulio Halperin-Donghi, "La revolución y la crisis de la estructura mercantil colonial en el Río de la Plata," in *Estudios de Historia Social,* 2 (Buenos Aires, 1966): 122.

chants" but adds that according to the evidence of several of the captains of the ships which carried Chilean copper to India, the big trading houses of Calcutta were willing to invest up to 200,000 pesos in breaking the monopoly of the English merchants of Coquimbo over the mines of northern Chile and "to place the system upon a fair and liberal footing" which seemed as remote in the postrevolutionary 1820s as it had been fifteen years earlier.[9]

Rather than allotting the blame for the prevailing situation, let us examine the basic outlook which at one stage or another guided the British traders in what Miers refers to as the practice of their trade. In flooding the Spanish American markets with British industrial goods, the British merchants were motivated by over-production in Great Britain and the mistaken notion that the newly opening market would undergo an intense and very prolonged process of expansion. While long-term planning was infrequent and not really necessary (in contrast to the period in which capital investment occupied an important place in the economic relation-ship between Great Britain and the new countries), the conduct of those who year after year overstocked the warehouses of Rio de Janeiro, Lima, Buenos Aires, and Valparaíso and who were obviously not setting out to ruin themselves reveals that they expected an indefinite period of expansion. Is this not the same principle underlying the attitude of the English merchants of Copiapó? As Hall noted, the merchants' profit would derive from the miner's increased production. But this too assumes a market eager to absorb the increased production of the mines.

It would be inaccurate to state that experience systematically disproved the theory of a constantly expanding market. In parts of Spanish America the market did appear to expand during the period following independence. For the foreign merchants, how-ever, even when faced with a reasonable chance of success, the consequences of miscalculation were too severe, and the policy of hedging the risks involved in dealing with an ever-fluctuating market by raising prices instead of raising the volume of imported goods became increasingly more tempting. In 1826 the British

9 Miers, *Travels,* II: 379.

consul in Lima was excited at the prospect of a future in which the British merchant would profit by "low prices on large dealings," support the abolition of trade restrictions, and militantly oppose contraband. In these expectations he was sadly alone. The British merchants enjoyed in fact "a species of monopoly . . . alike injurious to all parties," which made them particularly vulnerable to the competition which the arrival of the French and North Americans would bring. Their true attitude toward contraband is betrayed by their refusal to divulge the extent of their trading operations to the consul, owing to the fact "that the whole system of the trade may be said to be corrupt."[10] They were reluctant to place in his possession and, as they feared, that of their rivals information which would implicitly incriminate them.

The substitution of a small Spanish merchant group by another equally closed group of English merchants was not the only change wrought by the years of sudden prosperity and sudden ruin which followed 1810. That period of creative disorder saw the introduction of at least two innovations which were to prove irreversible. One was the increased consumption of imported industrial goods, which was to cause chronic problems of trade balance. The other was the very rapid dissipation of the extremely limited capital accumulated in Spanish America up to 1810. This capital stock may have solved the needs of a very static economy but would in any case have proved inadequate when commercial freedom stimulated an expansion of production for the overseas markets.

The negative aspects of the first of these two innovations are receiving more and more attention from Latin American scholars, but their critical fire is often misdirected. The inflow of imported low-cost goods was a very heavy blow to certain sectors of local production, particularly agriculture and handicrafts, but its effects were felt more gradually and partially than the apocalyptic versions of today's critics would have us believe. Thus, while the native cotton-weaving industry held its own in the areas of production and only barely lost its place in the commercial trading

[10] R. H. Humphreys, *British Consular Reports on the Trade and Politics of Latin America* (London, 1940), pp. 108, 126, 141.

circuits of Spanish America, woolens competed more successfully with British imports because the technology which was to drastically reduce the cost of production was not introduced until the middle of the nineteenth century.

By the same token, reform of the customs laws could not by itself immediately open the vast hinterland of Latin America to new imports. As noted by Miguel Urrutia M., "in the first half of the nineteenth century the protection which the tariffs gave to the artisans of eastern Colombia was far less efficient than that afforded by the topography of the country itself."[11] Together with the high cost of internal transportation, consideration should be given to the peculiar situation of those areas which were not geared to a monetary economy and had then no alternative but to consume their own production. (Such was the case in many among the traditional strongholds of the handicraft industries.)

If the effect of the extreme pressure of imports on some marginal sectors of the Spanish American economy has been exaggerated, insufficient attention has been paid to the effect of this pressure on the economy as a whole. Let us focus for a moment on some of the increasing difficulties experienced by the foreign trade sector, which had become dominant in the new economic structure as a result of the increased import of perishable consumer goods. Imports increased not only to replace local production but in answer to new consumer demand from a group much larger than the old colonial elite. (Obviously it was not the greater avidity of the elite for luxury goods which fueled the rapid expansion of cheap cotton textile imports during the first half of the century.) The comments of a French observer about Buenos Aires in 1825 might be made of a large part of Spanish America: the bill for imports became overwhelming because the population as a whole had given itself over to the consumption of superfluous articles. This conclusion does not, however, take into account that much of what were once considered superfluous items had become necessities with the passage of time. In Buenos Aires, after Indepen-

---

[11] Miguel Urrutia M., *Historia del sindicalismo en Colombia* (Bogotá, 1959), p. 38.

dence, Mariquita Sánchez could recall with disdainful compassion the time when all the members of a family drank from the same goblet; when the viceroy borrowed additional tableware for ceremonial banquets from his guests; when the shoes, even of elegantly dressed ladies, were of "an ordinary sheepskin and evil-smelling" and had to be stitched by these same ladies. It had been a time when it was not frowned upon to replace windowpanes with paper, since glass panes were always scarce, when butter was also scarce and foul-smelling ("It was the English," she said, "who taught us to make butter") and candles were of equally stinking tallow. Looking beyond her own social group she would recall that "the poor people went barefoot" and were, of course, extremely ill-clad.[12]

Even if modernization of the style of life did not necessarily give rise to an extravagant frenzy of consumption, this apparently irresistible urge of the private individual to spend more and, abetted by the pandering of eager salesmen, the changed patterns of consumption of the new states had important economic and social consequences.

The previously mentioned dispersion of the capital which should have been available for any future economic expansion was a consequence of this new trend in consumer spending. The process of dispersion, as contemporaries were aware, was complex. According to Charles Milner Ricketts, the British consul in Lima, between 1819 and 1825 British men-of-war alone carried off 26,900,-000 silver pesos' worth of gold and silver from Peru. This sum was only in part profits of British merchants. It included the capital of Spaniards and Creoles who were evading exactions of the local authorities and the risks inherent in their country's situation. Governments disposed of part of the funds they managed to obtain in the same way, and "the riches of Peru thus gradually disappeared, part having been drawn to Spain, part having been received by England, and the remainder having been dispersed by payment to the naval armaments and to the troops of Buenos Aires, Chile, and Colombia." While accurate in describing the fate of the money

---

[12] M. Sánchez, *Recuerdos* (Buenos Aires, 1953), pp. 26–33.

thus expatriated, this description gives a distorted version of the measure in which funds were thus absorbed.

To begin with, only in Mexico and Peru were large sums of money withdrawn and sent to Spain or Cuba. Second, the use of far larger sums in covering military expenses had economic consequences which Consul Ricketts failed to investigate. Only an insignificant portion of these expenses covered purchase of ships and armaments abroad; a greater, though still not the most important, part was used to pay local merchants for imported goods such as cloth for uniforms, and the largest portion covered payment of soldiers' salaries or the cost of locally produced goods such as food, cattle, horses, and harness. Indirectly, however, even these expenses contributed to stimulate imports. The army took the reserves of the churches, convents, lay corporations, and merchants (not always Spanish or politically disaffected) and distributed them among a far wider mass of potential consumers with preferences for the new range of products placed within their reach by freedom of trade. Thus, the limited sources of capital, enlarged by military contributions, were exhausted in increasing the flow of imports, and the hoarded treasures of which the army made use, and which had constituted a potential source of capital, became unavailable just at the moment in which commercial liberation offered suitable opportunities for investment.

The result of this situation, according to the concise résumé made by Ricketts in Peru, was that in spite of all that was said against the Spanish "between the years 1790 and 1800, there existed in Lima a *commercial* capital of over 15 millions of dollars; whereas in the present year it is under one million."[13] The consequences of this increasing penury were widespread. It hampered severely the expansion of production: in 1845 the Venezuelan Fermín Toro summed up the situation admirably, remarking that "the most notable difference" between the expansion of cocoa cultivation in colonial Venezuela and that of coffee after the wars of independence was that during the former period "agriculture could secure capital for investment at 5 percent per

[13] Humphreys, *Trade and Politics,* pp. 114–116.

annum, whereas the rate has subsequently risen to 1 percent and 2 percent per month."[14]

The same rates of interest were prevalent elsewhere. In Buenos Aires the consul of Sardinia observed during the forties that "la parola usura qui non ha senso" (the word "usury" has no meaning here).[15] The consequences of this situation were felt most directly by traders rather than producers. Commerce held a fever course: since high rates of interest made it impossible to keep large stocks in the hope of eventually selling for a profit, the pressure to liquidate stocks increasingly favored more abrupt and brutal variations in local prices. This was not, however, the main reason why the British traders could not enjoy their hegemony with the same serenity as their Spanish predecessors. The majority of the British traders were consignees, and although a negative balance during too long a period might cause their trade partners in England to stop remitting them goods, they were not directly affected by price variations. Their greatest risk came from the credit operations from which they could not refrain without losing buyers among the smaller merchants. Concerning the probity of the latter, opinions differed greatly, but they were singularly ill-adapted to face the brutal ups and downs of a small market, and not only economic but also political fluctuations directly affected their sales. Insolvency was frequent, and both the law and Spanish American commercial practice took a lenient view of bankruptcy, to the horror of the Europeans. Prudence, then, appeared more desirable than ever to the latter, who, repenting of their original optimism, limited the volume of their offers and based their prices on a generous margin of profit, commensurate with their risks. The new rulers of the market were thus condemned by the economic situation to the very monopoly whose dangers Ricketts had foreseen.

The British merchants in Spanish America were further influenced in their course by certain aspects of British economy. They

---

[14] Fermín Toro, "La doctrina conservadora," *Pensamiento politico venezolano del siglo XIX,* I (Caracas, 1960): 210.

[15] For a similar situation in Mexico see H. G. Ward, *Mexico in 1827,* I (London, 1828): 328.

had, from the outset, exceptionally close ties with British industry itself, either because manufacturers had organized the shipments and personally selected someone suitable to dispose of them in the newly opened markets or because the merchants themselves, returning from a successful expedition, directly contacted manufacturers for certain products, as was the case of the Robertson brothers after their first commercial trip to the Río de la Plata.[16] This close intimacy finally diminished as the great British import and export houses came to the fore, but the change did not affect the role of the British merchants in Spanish America insofar as they remained the emissaries of an essentially industrial economy and had to behave accordingly. Their interest in ensuring a relatively constant flow of predetermined goods arose in part from the fact that an industrial economy was less capable than a predominantly mercantile one of adapting to abrupt changes. For these reasons, the British traders found themselves increasingly conforming to the Spanish way of trade so decried in Spanish America. Their position became more and more ambiguous, and it becomes easier to understand why they tended increasingly to praise the very Spanish regime to whose overthrow they owed their own positions. The British attitude toward the incomplete character of freedom of trade in Spanish America sums up the situation precisely. No British merchant explicitly opposed freedom of trade, and British diplomats expressed themselves strongly in its favor, but at the same time it was already apparent that further advances in this direction did not altogether favor British interests.

In Chile the national monopoly of the coastal trade and the system of prohibition which made Coquimbo the northernmost port open to overseas trading was regarded by the British as prejudicial, increasing costs and diminishing the profits of the miners and at the same time depriving the British of a legitimate opportunity for trade, but in Mexico the consequences of opening up new ports to international trade were even more alarming to the British, who "repeated the error committed by the Spanish," establishing themselves in only one central point—the capital city

---

16 Humphreys, *Trade and Politics*, p. 126.

instead of Veracruz—and attempting to supply the vast and disparate Mexican market from there.[17] The result of this policy was that with the opening of Tampico, Soto la Marina, and Refugio, northeastern Mexican trade fell into the hands of the North Americans. The same thing happened on the Mexican Pacific Coast, where American merchants supplied Guadalajara from San Blas, the mining center of Sinaloa from Mazatlán, and Sonora and Chihuahua from Guaymas.

The contrast between the multiplicity of the lines of North American commercial penetration and the loyalty of the British to the traditional mercantile core of New Spain is directly related to the different conditions of their respective national economies. The English established themselves in the capital and tried to control commerce with the entire country from that point in order to reduce distribution expenses. They were forced to do so by the "great competition" which had depressed local prices of imported goods. The problem of excessive imports, producing a glut on the market and imposing the use of an inefficient but relatively inexpensive system of distribution on the importers, arose precisely because the British traders were forced to adjust to the rhythm of the industrial economy of their country.

In the ports of the north and of the Pacific, the North Americans were successfully selling, among other things, British goods. They were able to do so because for them this was only a sideline in a complex operation which could be readjusted to cope with conditions in the different markets they were covering. And while they too were acting partly as emissaries of the productive economies of their country (dealing mainly in flour and those rough but cheap domestic cloths which seriously competed with the British cottons during the 1820s), what was most important was their role in transport and trading, which allowed them to move with an agility which their British rivals could admire but not emulate.

In the long run the North American policy was not as successful as it appeared to be at first. Toward 1830 the competition which had momentarily alarmed the British traders and diplomats

[17] Ward, *Mexico,* I: 320–322.

appeared to fade away spontaneously almost everywhere, and it became apparent that British caution was better suited than American audacity to the peculiarities of the emergent independent Spanish American nations. The veritable mercantile revolution which accompanied independence brought about the establishment of a relationship between Spanish America and the new trading centers overseas which was in many aspects very different from that established with Spain before 1810 but which had one essential characteristic in common with it—it was scarcely dynamic. Once the initial expansion of the Spanish American consumer market was spent, the very circumscribed booms in economic production induced by commercial liberalization slowed down or stopped altogether, and once that had occurred the mercantile system based on the forecast of a future very similar to the present proved the winner.

The limited character of the stimulus offered by commercial liberalization to production was the deciding factor in shaping in independent Spanish America an economic order which disappointed the fiery hopes of the revolutionaries. Their plans had been based on the too simple assumption that only the commercial restrictions placed by Spain on colonial trade prevented the rapid growth of the Spanish American export economy. Subsequently it became apparent that this was not quite the case. In the first place, as we have seen, the interest of those who were early attracted to Spanish America was in selling rather than in buying. This circumstance alone was, however, not decisive, since the very arrival of foreign merchandise left many empty holds available which it would have been uneconomical to send home in ballast. For this reason, if for no other, foreign traders looked for local goods to export even when the profit was slender. Furthermore, lack of enthusiasm for local goods was not a valid argument in the case of precious metals, which were the most important export of almost all the Spanish American countries prior to Independence. It was precisely the extraction of precious metals, however, which suffered most in postrevolutionary times.

In this case, the expansion of production was more seriously impeded by shortage of capital than by limited demand. The original causes of this local scarcity have already been pointed out. The reasons for the worsening of the situation once the wars of independence were over are complex; the unsatisfactory situation of production was bound to make it increasingly difficult to accumulate capital in that sector; furthermore, the merchants who retained a smaller but still extremely important part of the profits on exports could be considered foreign not only because the most important among them were indeed recent immigrants but—even more important—because the merchandise they dealt in was still owned by British and European exporters. Thus, in one form or another, part of the profit derived from almost all commercial transactions, even in the domestic market, found its way overseas. On the other hand, the great risks involved made local investors reluctant to put their capital into the production sector of the economy. Simón Bolívar, who had great holdings in urban and rural property and who also owned mines said to be of enormous potential, would gladly have exchanged all for funds invested in England. As he wrote to his sister María Antonia, "we own too many properties and farms and houses which tomorrow will tumble in an earthquake . . . had we in England a hundred thousand pounds safely assured in the bank, we would enjoy an income of 3 percent per annum." And to his "Dear Peñalver" he added, "in my situation it would be more profitable to have in England four or five hundred thousand pesos in ready cash than to own a mine which neither I nor my family are able to work."[18] Years later Flora Tristán recorded the regrets of the Tristán and Goyeneche families of Arequipa, that they had not followed the example of that member of the clan who left Peru with his riches and was living affluently in Spain while those who had remained, among them a general and a bishop, both rich in their own right, had seen their income reduced and their capital threatened by the economic and political upheavals.

While it was tempting to draw capital out of an economic game

18 Bolívar to María Antonia, Potosí, October 24, 1825; Bolívar to Peñalver, Potosí, October 17, 1825, Bolívar, *Obras completas,* I (Havana, 1947): 1215.

fraught with dangers, it was perhaps equally tempting to invest it at a high risk in the hope of obtaining extraordinary profits. Both risk and profit were enormous in lending to the indigent new states. From Mexico to Montevideo the so-called *agiotistas* appeared, specializing in short-term loans, frequently at extortionate terms, to governments whose needs for funds were insatiable. These loans gave the creditors considerable influence over the young governments, enabling them to profit in ways not directly related to the loans themselves. Parallel to such shady financial arrangements, speculation became rife; and even gambling, to which the monotony of existence reduced cities and military encampments alike, came to be regarded by those not altogether destitute as a normal economic activity. If we are to believe the evidence of the venomous General Iriarte, in 1819 some eminent merchants of Buenos Aires who had found in gambling a profitable activity had ordered in Rio de Janeiro a set of dice ingeniously loaded with mercury. This story, which may or may not be apocryphal, sheds a crude light on the economic and moral confusion among the elite, some of whose members, while not necessarily cheats, were responsible for organizing a gambling den without, apparently, losing either their personal respectability or their commercial prestige.

Lack of capital combined with timidity made local investors reluctant to become involved in productive activities, while foreigners were no more adventuresome. Only those sectors of production requiring a small investment could therefore expand after the wars of independence. Thus, while the mining industry declined or even came to a halt in some regions, cattle raising flourished, and similar though less extreme contrasts can be discovered between different agricultural activities.

From Mexico to Bolivia mining was, in fact, the source of the greatest disappointments. In Mexico war created profound dislocations in the labor market and brought about a deterioration of the mines themselves. In some cases they became flooded owing to the destruction of their drainage systems; the same deterioration was apparent in the rural metal-refining establishments. An additional and appreciable cause of their decay lay in the shortage of capital brought about by the collapse of the credit system, "which it had required three centuries to bring to the state of perfection in which it existed at the commencement of the War of Independence."[19] This, despite the fact that Mexico was the only country in Latin America to attract European, predominantly British, investors to its mines: the machinery brought in by the new companies was puny alongside the impressive ruins of the old prerevolutionary mines. It is then not surprising that Mexican exports of precious metals shrank from 21 million pesos during the period between 1795 and 1810 to 9 million pesos between 1825 and 1851.[20] By the middle of the century slow but steady progress brought exports up to the prewar level, demonstrating that mining had once again become a profitable business.[21] Even so, and in spite of the fact that remittances to the royal treasury (which in colonial times had absorbed one-third of these exports) were no longer required, mining exports were insufficient to cover the cost of increased imports, and the mining industry could no longer offer the exchequer a source of revenue equivalent to that of the latter colonial period. Under these circumstances, notwithstanding diplomat Sir Henry George Ward's optimistic projections, it could hardly have been expected that the Mexican mining industry, which was slowly getting back onto its feet, could play a revitalizing role in the national economy as a whole.[22] Ward (a shrewd if not always disinterested observer) had hoped that the reviving prosperity of the mines would alleviate the lack of capital and restore interest rates to levels which would allow long-term investments in the agricultural sector, but contrary to his forecast, the mines were still taking up an excessive share of the available capital and inhibiting development of other sectors of the economy as late as the middle of the century.[23]

In Peru the mining industry appears to have followed a substantially similar course.[24] The available data on the silver refinery of Cerro de Pasco between 1825 and 1836 show that recovery was

[19] Ward, *Mexico*, II: 57.

[20] *Ibid.*, pp. 13–14.

[21] F. López Cámara, *La estructura económica y social de México* (Mexico, 1967), p. 78.

[22] Ward, *Mexico*, I: 328.

[23] López Cámara, *La estructura económica*, p. 71.

[24] Archibald Smith, *Peru as It Is*, II (London, 1839): 27.

relatively steady, but slow. Even in 1836 the amount of silver worked at the refinery suggests that production was only a little more than half what it had been prior to 1810 (which agrees with the estimates of Adolf Soetbeer).[25] The lack of information regarding the vicissitudes of mining in the postrevolutionary period, compared with the attention paid to the crisis and slow recovery of coastal agriculture and to the sudden boom of the guano and nitrate industries, is direct evidence of the ineffectiveness of silver production in bolstering the Peruvian economy as a whole. The situation in the Bolivian mines was comparable. From 1806, when war in Europe caused a crisis in the supply of mercury, followed by the still greater crisis of Spanish American independence, production remained static until the middle of the century and was once again only half what it had been prior to the revolution.[26] It should, moreover, be borne in mind that in the Peruvian area, in contrast to Mexico, production had already begun to drop perceptibly prior to the revolution. Similarly, the production of gold in Nueva Granada dropped abruptly after the revolution, improving after 1840 and attaining prerevolutionary levels of production only after 1850.[27]

Chile was the only Spanish American country in which the mining industry grew noticeably after the revolution. After 1820 copper became an important export staple, and by 1860 Chile was the world's leading exporter of this mineral. The discovery of silver in Chañarcillo in 1831 led to an even more rapid development, and by 1850 production of silver was almost five times greater than in the heyday of the empire (it is true that gold production, which had exceeded that of silver prior to 1810, decreased considerably because the richer sources of this mineral were now nearly exhausted).[28] The reasons for the Chilean success provide understanding of the failure of more traditional centers. Chile had the advantage of a system of transport and marketing which placed

[25] A. Soetbeer, *Edel-metall Produktion* (Gotha, 1879), p. 69.
[26] L. Peñaloza, *Historia económica de Bolivia,* II (La Paz, 1954): 10.
[27] Soetbeer, *Edel-metall Produktion,* p. 63.
[28] *Ibid.,* p. 82.

productive mines within easy access of the ports opened to overseas trade after 1810. This factor was decisive in the case of copper, in which access to the markets of India played a crucial role. Labor was also plentiful: reserves of labor in the rural areas of central Chile were culturally far less isolated than in Andean Peru, and capitalists and workers with mining experience, refugees from the recurrent civil wars of the Andean provinces of Argentina, were also readily available. The final and possibly the most decisive factor, however, was that Chilean deposits were less costly to mine than the overworked mines of Mexico and Peru. Hence, the shortage of capital was less of an impediment.

High costs, scarcity of capital, and labor troubles were regarded as the three basic causes of stagnation in the mining industry elsewhere in Latin America. The first of these particularly affected the mining and refining of silver and was only in part due to working exhausted seams (reduced production led, on the contrary, to concentration on the richer ones). The use of mercury in refining silver, following an antiquated process instituted in colonial times, contributed greatly to increased costs, since mercury was expensive and always in short supply. In Mexico distance added yet more to its price, and in Peru the same problem, combined with the drop in the production of mercury at Huancavelica, increased it further still. Shortage of capital everywhere played a decisive part in maintaining a technological backwardness which, however much deplored, was impossible to correct without large investments.

Labor problems were of varying importance in the different mining regions of Spanish America. Already at the peak of the mining period in the eighteenth century, Mexico relied on paid labor, the prosperity of the period allowing the workers a slightly better wage than in European mines, and in this respect the situation did not vary substantially after the revolution.[29] Even in Peru, shortage of labor was not serious. Indian labor was so abundant that only the larger silver refining establishments used

[29] Ward, *Mexico,* II: 145–147; López Cámara, *La estructura económica,* p. 224.

mules to tread the mixture of silver and mercury. The *bolicheros,* small-scale merchants, employed Indians "who trod the mercury for hours to mix it with the silver," and in spite of financing their activities with credit loans at high interest rates they managed by "exploiting the Indian in every possible way . . . to amass considerable fortunes in the space of a very few years."[30] In Bolivia, although the *mita,* enforced Indian labor, had been abolished, the daily wage of the workers in the middle of the nineteenth century was 4 reales per day and thus no higher than that of the *mitayos* in 1606 and lower than the daily wage of the free workers of the same prosperous era who supplemented the forced work of the *mita* Indians.[31] It was only in Nueva Granada, where slave labor was used in mining gold, that the ban put on importing slaves, although attenuated by contraband, decisively affected the mining industry. We can conclude therefore that the one prevailing adverse factor responsible for the decay of the mining industry was the scarcity of capital which everywhere accentuated the effects of technical backwardness. Shortages of labor were far less frequent.

The development of agriculture and cattle raising, on the other hand, was most successful where the investment required was modest. Thus, one of the first Spanish American countries to enter a successful period of reconstruction was Venezuela, which was also one of the areas most devastated and impoverished by war. Here, where in 1828 landowners, anxious to return to production, accepted loans at rates as high as 15 percent per month, the process of reconstruction was remarkable, particularly in the cultivation of coffee, which replaced cocoa as the principal export.[32] The isolation brought about by war had made the former commodity preferable, since it could be stored over longer periods and was more attractive to the foreign markets which, legally or not, began to replace the Spanish one. "All the new plantations established since 1796," observed Depons in 1806, "are of coffee . . . but it must not be thought that this product has already

[30] J. J. von Tschudi, *Testimonio del Perú* (Lima, 1966), p. 260.
[31] Peñaloza, *Historia,* I: 208; II: 101.
[32] R. Veloz, *Economia y finanzas de Venezuela* (Caracas, 1945), p. 16.

achieved the full expansion of which it is capable."[33] At this time the coffee exported was estimated at a million pounds per annum. During the postwar period, progress was more rapid. In 1831–1832 the volume of exports doubled and became ten times greater than it had been in prewar years. In the following decade it once again tripled. From that time on, however, world prices became subject to frequent and violent fluctuations, and growth slowed.[34]

Coffee cultivation was carried out nearly always by free men rather than slaves on land other than their own. The landowner supplied land to the cultivator, who paid him for the same in work and in produce, the owner thus dispensing with payment of money wages or the more onerous burden of purchasing and replacing slaves with which the cocoa producers were faced. According to Fermín Toro, in 1841–1842[35] the expansion of the coffee-growing industry signified an investment of 10 million pesos, spread over half a century, while for Agustín Codazzi, the total capital value of land and improvements in the enterprises engaged in coffee production was approximately 19 million pesos in 1839.[36] (It should, however, be borne in mind that Codazzi was dealing with the value of the plantations at that juncture rather than making a retrospective estimate of investments.)

Taking as a point of departure the date supplied by Toro and the local value of coffee exports as stated by Ramón Veloz, the total of 330,000 quintals of coffee exported in 1841–1842 amounted to well over 4,000,000 pesos, of which, always presuming the calculations of Toro to be correct, the producers would have received approximately 2,700,000. These are of course extremely approximate estimates which can be used only to give some indication of the magnitude of the profits to be found in coffee (about 27 percent per annum), but the fact that the expansion of the coffee plantations involved credit loans at the rate of 18

---

[33] François Raymond Joseph Depons, *Voyage à la partie orientale de la Terre-Ferme, dans L'Amérique Méridio nale*, II (Paris: Colnet, 1806): 231.

[34] Veloz, *Economia*, pp. 40, 70.

[35] Toro, "La doctrina conservadora," pp. 211–212.

[36] A. Codazzi, *Resumen de la geografía de Venezuela* (Caracas, 1940), pp. 348–349.

percent per annum and a wait of two or three years for the first crop implies that this expansion could have been viable only at rates of profit not far below those mentioned above.[37]

Whatever the comparative advantages of cultivating coffee, they were small in comparison to those afforded by investing in cattle. The annual yield on the Venezuelan cattle exports was calculated at almost 3,700,000 pesos by Codazzi. It is true that to the haciendas devoted to cattle raising he assigned a capital value of 15,000,000 pesos, thus presuming a gross yield of around 25 percent, but it should be recalled that of this value 80 percent was represented by the cattle themselves, more than 10 percent being accounted for by the land, and only about 8 percent (1,120,000 pesos) represented investment in cash in relatively recent periods.[38] Again, only the newcomers had to use ready cash to acquire land and cattle, and the annual rate of slaughter not only ensured preservation of the stock but also permitted it to increase rapidly. In other words, while the estimates of Codazzi accurately weigh the different factors related to production, he is not concerned with the fluctuations in income and expenditure on the part of the individual landowner who contributed to revive cattle raising after the war and whose success depended on the reestablishment of internal order and growing contacts with foreign markets rather than on fresh capital investment.

The development of agriculture in Venezuela was paralleled by similar developments in the extreme south of Spanish America, in Chile, and above all in some of the Argentine provinces. In Chile, following a crisis in grain production in the early 1820s (which was not entirely due to climatic causes), expansion was hampered by new difficulties of access to the most important traditional foreign market, Peru. In the following decade the situation became more favorable. The growth of the internal market, which was a result, above all, of the flourishing mines of Norte Chico, and the victory over Peru and Bolivia in 1839 (which entailed the consequent reopening of the Lima market), was followed ten years later

[37] *Ibid.*, p. 148.
[38] *Ibid.*, pp. 184, 350.

by the creation of new markets in the mining centers of the Pacific, from California to Australia, which lent a fevered rhythm to expansion, halted only in 1869 by the increase of local production in those overseas markets. Cattle raising also became more important: from 1830 onward, numerous salting houses were established along the coast near Valparaíso, although hides still remained the main staple export of the cattle-raising industry. By midcentury the export trade in cattle products in the Southern Pacific had become sufficiently intense to attract cattle sellers from the Andean and central provinces of neighboring Argentina.[39]

The growth of cattle raising in Argentina took place within a more limited area than in Chile, and the enormous contrast between the increasing prosperity of that area and the chronic weakness of the economy of the remainder of the country became one of the basic features of national life. In the forty years between 1810 and 1850 exports of cattle products from Buenos Aires increased more than ten times. Cattle came mostly from the immediate hinterland of the port of Buenos Aires, which in colonial times had been regarded as an area weak in this respect. This was brought about because the traditional cattle tracts of colonial times, the Banda Oriental (which became the Republic of Uruguay in 1830) and the provinces of Entre Ríos, Corrientes, and Santa Fé, underwent a long cycle of wars starting in 1810 and prolonged by new internal and international conflicts which brought about a systematic destruction of the herds, from which Santa Fé began to recover only after 1830, Entre Ríos and Corrientes ten years later, and Uruguay (after a couple of promising starts which were brutally interrupted by the return of war) only in the second half of the century. The elimination of competition from those particularly well-favored areas was not, however, the only positive influence. The city of Buenos Aires played an equally vital part. By the end of the colonial period the city had become the trading center for the whole of southern Spanish America, which the revolution had cut off from its most important suppliers, among them Alto

39 Note from Justo Maeso in Woodbine Parish, *Buenos Aires* (Buenos Aires, 1958), pp. 490–491.

Peru and Chile, sources of the precious metals which until 1810 constituted more than 80 percent of its exports. The merchant class of the city of Buenos Aires, affected by the loss of supplies from those areas and by the competition afforded by the arrival of foreign merchants, sought new sources of profits in cattle breeding, and after 1820 the government of the province of Buenos Aires placed the resources obtained from levying customs duties on the international trade of all the Argentine provinces at the almost exclusive service of developing Buenos Aires's rural industry.

While the financial and political resources of Buenos Aires, which ten years of war and extravagance had not entirely dissipated, made possible the rapid expansion of cattle raising, the economic attractions of this activity were the deciding factor in its development. The expenses of reclaiming much of the land from the aborigines after 1810, involving costly campaigns, were met by the state with resources derived from import tariffs and thus neither directly nor indirectly affected the landowning cattle raisers; when this source of revenue proved insufficient, paper money was issued, once again striking a blow mainly at certain sectors of the urban economy. Furthermore, while the process of acquiring reclaimed land from the government was both long and complex, the new owners never had to pay high prices for the lands placed at their disposal.

Cattle raising carried out on an extensive scale made technical improvements superfluous, and this obviated the necessity of large investments except for the acquisition of the cattle themselves, with which to initiate the venture. As in Venezuela, the very low initial investment was a great attraction, at least as important as the profits which in "normal" years (i.e., taking into account the optimistic prejudice of contemporary observers who so classified them, exceptionally good years) rose to more than 30 percent of the original investment. This provided the incentive for an expansion which, in spite of wars, drawn-out political crises, blockades, and drought, raised the total exports of cattle products of the province of Buenos Aires from a sum a little below 200,000 pounds in 1810 to 2,000,000 pounds in 1850 and contributed to doubling the size of the territories held by the province of Buenos Aires.

In the Río de la Plata, as in Venezuela, the expansion of the postrevolutionary export trade was yet further encouraged by the fact that the area already possessed a relatively complex marketing system which prior to 1810 placed it in direct contact with overseas markets. To a certain extent this encouraged the production of traditional and new goods, the first and uncertain stages of expansion having been protected (before increased productivity brought about a new and vigorous export trade) by the foreign merchants' need to obtain returns on their own country's produce.

The phenomenon of impressive postrevolutionary development in an area which had been very much cut off prior to 1810 was observed only in Chile. Here good fortune favored the country by reducing the royalist forces earlier than in Peru and making Valparaíso the unexpected center for British shipping and trade for the whole of the South American Pacific. The establishment of merchants and warehouses in Chile was thus the result of war rather than a colonial heritage. It should, however, be remembered that both merchants and warehouses existed in Chile prior to the period of postwar reconstruction and that in those countries where they were conspicuously absent the new export economies met with little success. Although all over Spanish America there were other areas potentially capable of a cattle-producing boom comparable to that which took place in the Río de la Plata and in Venezuela, for which the only requisite was tolerably flat and empty land, the fact remains that there was no parallel expansion elsewhere. John L. Stephens records that he saw the owners of vast territories along the coasts of the Central American Pacific, with more cattle than they could count, living in penury amid potential wealth. Success was thus far more difficult but not impossible to achieve where there was no previous merchant organization. Thus, on the plain of San José de Costa Rica, Stephens witnessed the beginning of the expansion of the coffee plantations, a result above all of the obstinate persistence of a small group of landowners whose neighbors prophesied their certain ruin, and in fact, here expansion only gradually led to new trade contacts overseas, since nothing had been prepared beforehand.[40]

Characteristic of the economic growth that took place in independent Spanish America was that it was still a partial, almost a marginal feature in a situation marked by widespread stagnation, and outright decline in some of the former economic centers of colonial times. Furthermore, even where growth took place, it faced apparently insuperable barriers born partly of the prudence of traders and producers alike, disillusioned more than once after 1810, but even more of the limited possibilities offered by international trade itself. Both were related to a lack of enthusiasm abroad for investing in Spanish America. This apathy ceased only briefly during the feverish years leading up to the 1825 crisis, when the future of Spanish America seemed momentarily open to vast developments, but the disillusionment of 1825 abruptly put an end to hope and served only to confirm and consolidate a concept of Spanish America and its place in the world which was only to be modified, and even then with great reluctance, in the second half of the century.

The reasons for this brief surge of foreign investments are complex. At a time when Latin America accounted for a quarter of the British exports sold to Europe, it appeared sensible practice to invest there when capital became available in London. Furthermore, since merchant interests lay in directing the policy of the British government toward the recognition of the new nations by means of the pressure of public opinion, they took to using as a lure the fabulous potential wealth of the new countries, drawing the attention of the public to the opportunities for investment there. Propaganda was carried out along very traditional lines, and it was above all the mineral wealth of Spanish America which was stressed. The fact that silver mining, or indeed any form of mining, included certain working costs, and that the profits would depend on the margin between such costs, which might be high, and the

40 L. B. Stephens, *Incidents of Travel,* I (New Brunswick, N.J., 1949): 300–301.

sale price of the metal extracted, was conveniently forgotten. An industry which at that particular stage of Spanish American history was not the most promising hence attracted investment not only because of the prestige of an already archaic image of Spanish America but also because of the peculiar situation of the European economy at the time, which was faced with a serious shortage of precious metal. Thus, for a variety of reasons, the greater part of the potential investors were attracted to mining ventures in Spanish America. The merciless propaganda campaign directed in London toward the unwary offered them a share in the rights to mines which could be immediately and profitably exploited. At least some of the organizers of the new mining ventures were fully aware that this was not really the case, but even they tended to exaggerate the necessity of introducing labor-saving innovations and new techniques. From Mexico to Peru and Buenos Aires a not insignificant part of the available funds were spent in recruiting and transporting miners from Germany or Cornwall to replace local labor, which was generally supposed to be inexpert and indolent. The results of this effort were disappointing. British miners in Mexico afforded an unedifying spectacle of insolent indolence and unbridled consumption of alcohol.[41] Even when their conduct was less reprehensible, their advantages over the much cheaper local labor were hardly apparent. Apart from anything else, they were incapable of the physical exertions of the latter in the high altitudes at which so many of the Spanish American mines were found.

Similar conclusions were reached after attempts to introduce new and more profitable techniques. Sometimes they were a total failure, since they failed to take into account the characteristics of the mineral for which they were intended, and even when this was not the case, the cost of these innovations as compared to the increase of productivity made them a doubtful asset. Ward himself, who not altogether disinterestedly defended the action of the British companies in the Mexican silver mines, was forced to admit that the transport of steam-powered machinery from Vera-

[41] Ward, *Mexico,* II: 432.

cruz to the mines of Regla had been extremely costly and that it would be a long time before the highway from the same mines to the processing plants of Real del Monte, which replaced the former mule track, would justify its exorbitantly high cost, even though carts were obviously a safer and less costly form of transport than mules.[42]

The optimism displayed by Ward was not altogether unfounded: although the British mining enterprises in Mexico deceived their investors into believing briefly that profits would be both immediate and high, they were responsible for a slow but real revival of the mining industry. Of southern Spanish American mining ventures the same cannot be said: none of the Anglo-South American enterprises survived the crisis of 1825, and they left hardly a trace on the history of mining itself. Again, the causes of failure were manifold: in some cases the fact that these ventures were launched at the later stages of the boom was in itself enough to account for failure, since the crisis took them by surprise before they were properly launched. (According to Edmond Temple, such was the case in Potosí.)[43] There was, however, a more systematic cause of failure: the decay of the traditional mining centers of South America, which was everywhere apparent, and the problematic future of new mining ventures, such as those of La Rioja in the Argentine provinces, which awoke the lively interest of the London investor. In this context, the speculative aspect of the wave of investments in Spanish America became of paramount importance. Perhaps nowhere was this so obvious as in the case of the Río de la Plata mines, precisely because nowhere was there less certainty of making a satisfactory return on investment by expansion of the workings.

Two companies were formed in London to work the mines of Famatina in La Rioja. One received the patronage of Bernardino Rivadavia, who was not only a diplomatic agent of the Buenos Aires government but also the most influential politician in the area. It was organized by Hullet Brothers, a mercantile house with

---

[42] *Ibid.*, 354–356.
[43] E. Temple, *Travels in . . . Peru,* I (London, 1830): 363–368.

longstanding connections in the Río de la Plata and Chile. The second was favored by the political rulers of the province of La Rioja, including the governor himself and the local political and military strong man, Juan Facundo Quiroga, and among its backers were some of the most influential Argentine and British merchants of the Río de la Plata area. The two enterprises competed rather to entice the British investor than to obtain control of the somewhat uncertain riches of Famatina. Eventually, hostilities between them, expressed in challenging notices in the London Stock Exchange and an acrimonious exchange of letters in the *Times,* prejudiced both, particularly the second, which was too late to make the most of the South American boom.[44] Regarding the potential of this undertaking, there appears to have been a certain amount of skepticism in the Río de la Plata itself. Rivadavia hastened to rid himself of the founder's shares assigned to him by the company under his auspices. The organizers of the rival concern, who, with the authorization of the helpful provincial authorities, had simultaneously established a mint in La Rioja, intended to import metal from Chile and Bolivia rather than rely on locally extracted material. The promoters of both companies appeared equally to share the feeling of Bolívar, who stated that the investments of the British in Spanish American mining enterprises merely proved that "the English capitalists . . . did not know what to do with their riches."[45]

In the midst of this wave of speculation it was hardly surprising that only a fraction of the proceeds of sale of shares in the mines on the London Stock Exchange should actually have been invested. But both these investments and part of the money gained by speculation (here some Spanish Americans revealed an inventiveness and audacity equal to that of their British allies or rivals) had an additional effect on the Spanish American economy as a whole, perhaps no less important than that which it had on the mining sector itself. When Ward calculated the market value of

---

[44] Tulio Halperin-Donghi, *Historia Argentina,* III (Buenos Aires, 1972): 263–268.

[45] Bolívar to his sister María Antonia. Potosí, October 24, 1825; Vargas, *Obras completas,* pp. 90–135.

effective British investments in the Mexican mines at 12 million pesos (or somewhat less than 2.5 million pounds), he hastened to add that the actual specie exported from Great Britain to Mexico "on mining account" did not exceed 300,000 pesos and that the 12 million pesos represented capital "which would, otherwise, have found its way to Europe" and which "in exchange for the Bills of the different companies" was permitted to remain in Mexico.[46] This capital would otherwise have left the country in payment for imports, and only a small portion would have contributed to the productive capacity of the mines. In other words, thanks to the boom in mining investments, Mexico was able, for the space of several years, to import consumer goods which it couldn't pay with its exports.

This more general and indirect effect of the wave of British investments became paramount in Spanish America, where the mining centers themselves, toward which the investments were ostensibly directed, were almost unaffected by them. The same general effect was even more clearly apparent insofar as loans to the governments of the new states were concerned. These generally unfortunate operations involved far greater sums than mining speculations. According to data supplied by Henry English and compiled by James Rippy, the Spanish American mining companies together had a capital of 3,258,500 pounds, of which the Mexican mines alone accounted for 2,213,500 pounds. The bonds of the different Latin American states were placed on the market at a nominal value of 18 million pounds and sold for more than 14 million pounds, of which perhaps 10 million found their way to Spanish America.[47] This sum was far more equally distributed among the different Spanish American countries than was the mining investment. Mexico and Gran Colombia each raised about 7 million pounds nominal value; Peru, about 2 million pounds; Chile and the province of Buenos Aires, a million each. The bonds covering the Mexican loan were sold for 3,000,732 pounds, and Mexico

---

[46] Ward, *Mexico,* II: 69.

[47] D. Bushnell, *The Santander Regime* (Newark, Del., 1954), pp. 119–121; Rippy, *British Investment,* p. 20.

received somewhat more than 2,800,000 pounds; of this sum more than half was used to cover current administrative expenses, a little less than a quarter went toward defraying arrears of debt, and the remainder to purchase arms and military equipment and (to maintain the state's monopoly thereon in spite of the disruptions wrought by war on its production and marketing) tobacco. Distribution took place elsewhere along similar lines. In Colombia the payment of arrears accounted for only a sixth of the 3,622,745 pounds received against a nominal issue of 6,750,000 pounds and placement proceeds of 5,883,150 pounds; less was spent here on tobacco and more on general expenses and war.[48] War expenses were also predominant in Peru and even more in Buenos Aires (the latter, having arranged the terms of its credit loan in a period of peace and prosperity, received it when already involved in ruinous war against the Brazilian empire).

While the mining ventures were recalled with displeasure principally by the British investors, the governmental loans were as unpopular in Spanish America as in London. Since by the end of the decade the debtor countries had defaulted, the launching of new credit transactions became, of course, totally impossible, and while it is true that some individuals in Britain had benefited from placing the original loans, they were careful to keep this fact from their victims, and what were mainly audible were the plaints of the prejudiced against the defaulting Spanish American governments. This was so partly because they acted through the banks which had been mainly responsible for offering the loans on the stock exchange, and which didn't relish attacks on themselves, partly because only the governments concerned could, by resuming payment for services rendered, restore some degree of value to the bonds which had been issued.

The recipient countries viewed matters differently. To begin with, the fact that the sum of money which they had received was not much over half the nominal value of the loans was regarded as shocking, particularly considering that the terms of the contract specified that their nominal value was to be taken for purposes of

[48] J. Bazant, *Historia de la deuda exterior de Mexico* (México, 1968), p. 27.

repayment. In some cases, the reasons behind such agreements were strictly honorable. The first loans, launched before the credit of the new nations was fully established, had to be placed on the market much below par. In the case of Mexico, Goldschmidt of London placed the bonds on the market at the rate of 58 percent of their nominal value and delivered 50 percent of their nominal value to the Mexican government.[49] Even so, subsequent price increases allowed speculation on later Mexican loan bonds, in which it is not improbable that the issuing banks participated, although no additional income was supplied to the Mexican state. The situation was not always so clear. Each separate loan was very soon the cause of complex accusations of corruption, with regard both to the transaction itself and to in-country investment (particularly in the case of repayment of the internal debt, where the all too frequent implication was that only those who were favored, gratuitously or otherwise, by the financial rulers of the country were likely to receive payment). Negotiations carried out at a distance, in London, were frequently regarded as shady. In Colombia the authorities flinched on receiving the latest European papers with bulletins on the most recent undertakings of their representative in London, who, for his part, was suspiciously remiss in keeping them informed.[50] In Chile the government accepted a loan on the insistence of an agent, Irrisarri, at an inopportune moment and at extortionate terms. The agent maintained that his negotiations had been carried out in the name of the Chilean Republic and that the credit of the country would suffer in the future if the terms he had agreed upon were not complied with, be they good or bad. The interest of the agents was understandable: even when their commissions did not exceed the normal percentage, this sum was a very attractive proposition. Commissions were, however, frequently higher, the most noteworthy case being that of the Buenos Aires loan. A government decree in 1823 authorized a loan to be contracted at the rate of 70 percent of the nominal value. At the height of the wave of speculation, the agents of

[49] Bushnell, *Santander,* p. 113.
[50] Miers, *Travels,* II: 382–385.

Buenos Aires in London (who were also the agents of the mining company favored by the government of La Rioja) received an offer of 85 percent from Baring Brothers. The offer was not as generous as it appeared, since it was easy to place the securities on the market at 94 percent. For their part, the agents accounted almost entirely for the difference of £150,000.

Quite apart from the question of financial morality, which was a source of indignation not untinged with envy in the impoverished Spanish American capitals, the very advisability of these operations became open to question. It was argued that Buenos Aires, whose resources were sufficient to cover the rising public expenditure of a period of economic growth, was rash in accepting a loan of a little over 500,000—on condition of repaying 1,000,000 plus interests. Doubts were even greater with regard to the more insolvent states. The impossibility of repaying loans destined for the most part to covering public expenditures in countries which did not appear able to increase their ordinary income in the near future became increasingly obvious. Cessation of payments appeared to be the almost inevitable consequence of loans whose sole advantage was that they offered the indigent nations an opportunity briefly to continue overspending.

It was the negative consequences of accepting loans, rather than the almost invariably disappointing results of the mining investments, which accounted for a growing coldness among Spanish Americans toward the British, who as merchants and investors had so easily dominated their market. When the sudden inflow of investment was abruptly cut off, the increased prosperity which it was hoped the revolution would bring about appeared to be further off than ever. The crisis of 1825 favored a more sober evaluation of the profits and losses brought about by the altered relationship of Spanish America to the world economy, and while foreign interests had become too powerful to be affected by this new attitude, the Spanish American bias in their favor disappeared completely, to return only after the middle of the century when the general growth of British and European economies once again altered the situation.

The new equilibrium led to conclusions which were similar in more than one respect to those learned from earlier lessons. Both the Spanish American governments and British investors learned above all that the period of rapid change was over. The newly established economic order brought about by the revolution could not easily be modified, whether it was acceptable or not, and recognition of this fact had important political and economic consequences: leaders who proposed difficult and daring reforms were eyed with a newborn distrust, while those who promised to consolidate, rather than to overturn the frail new order, were welcomed. In 1824 the British consul, Woodbine Parish, together with all enlightened citizens of Buenos Aires, could deplore the end of the term of office of Bernardino Rivadavia, the minister whose reforms had brought about impressive progress to the province of Buenos Aires in the space of a mere three years. Two years later Parish was condemning the lack of common sense, prudence, and political morality which, as he now felt, were characteristic of Rivadavia. Three years after that Parish, scandalously forgetful of his obligation to remain neutral in the face of internal conflicts, celebrated the first advances of the troops of Juan Manuel de Rosas, prosperous landowner and man of business, who had been skillful enough to gather, from among the masses and the business sector, a following for his proposed campaign, whose essential purpose was turning the clock back.

Thus, even for the dominant metropolitan economy, the crisis marked the end of an illusion. The Spanish America which had emerged from the crisis of independence was not always regarded with great sympathy. A number of British merchants learned bitter lessons from their experiences in Spanish America, lessons as bitter as those derived in Spanish America from the consequences of their entrepreneurial energy. Violent disapproval in principle of the emerging Spanish American economic order was now accompanied by the admission that for anyone seeking for prosperity rather than ruin in Spanish America it was essential to make use of whatever advantages existing circumstances offered rather than to attempt to alter them.

Of this attitude, so uncertain in its motives and so clear in its objectives, John Miers gives an especially sound account in his

Chilean memoirs. He had not the slightest appreciation for Chile or its inhabitants. According to him, all Chileans were born thieves, even the ladies of Valparaíso used to steal the jewels of the English residents who were imprudent enough to display them, and the governor himself had a piece of furniture whose elegance he admired stolen from the house of an English resident and transferred to his daughter's drawing room. The only restraint on this national instinct for theft was fear of the brutal and arbitrary punishment inflicted by the law of the times. Nothing was more dangerous, according to Miers, than to attribute any significance to the charming welcome accorded by the Chileans to foreigners, since this was but one more sign of their polished hypocrisy. Their superstitious religion could not but appear repulsive to an enlightened observer, and their servility toward the politically powerful, stronger even than their faith tarnished with superstition, kindled Miers's disdain. Not even their mode of dress went uncondemned. The care with which the members of the Santiago elite dressed seemed to him as worthy of reproof as the poor apparel of the lower classes and countryfolk. But when this persistently misanthropic witness paused to examine mining (in which he himself was involved), his tone altered considerably. The foreigner arriving in Chile and witnessing the backwardness of local techniques might well judge that rapid modernization was required. He would learn eventually to his cost that many of the practices which appeared absurd were those which ensured the best use of the plentiful and hence low-cost resources locally available and which reduced to a minimum the use of those which were scarce and hence unduly expensive.

On arrival in Chile, Miers, just another of the foreigners drawn by the myth of Spanish American riches, had proposed "to erect a very extensive train of machinery . . . for refining, rolling and manufacturing copper into shearing" using Chilean coal. He ended up by advising others to be less ambitious. Since the Chileans knew how to mine in the most economical manner in their own setting, mining should be left to them, and capital should be advanced to them as the *habilitadores* had been doing for centuries. Even in this limited role, Miers advised the British capitalist to be circumspect. An investment far smaller than the immense sums frequently mentioned in London by would-be investors could irreparably damage a system geared to a chronic shortage of capital.

The economic arguments with which Miers sought to bolster his advice are not too convincing. He feared above all that the greater availability of capital might affect the labor market, either directly by causing salary increases, should supplies of labor not increase together with demand, or indirectly, if supply were to increase owing to the relocation of former agricultural workers. The latter, by becoming consumers rather than producers, would increase the price of food, which would, in turn, affect wage levels. Although these arguments can be refuted (Miers overlooked hidden unemployment in the countryside),[51] the confidence with which he adhered to the economic formula of being prodigal with that which was abundant and cheap (labor and ore), and reducing other expenses to a minimum, was due less to his unfortunate incursions into the realm of economic theory than to his own experiences in Chile.

Thus the scarcity of metropolitan capital available for investment in Latin America was not only recognized as a fact but declared to be a necessary condition for the success of the British investor in Spanish America and the benefit of the area in which investment was to take place. This conclusion is closely related to the notion that Britain's too energetic efforts to revive local economies were dangerous to the frail Spanish American nations. In this respect, the conclusion reached after the brief surge of investments ending in 1825 condensed and confirmed those accumulated over the previous fifteen years.

Was this wisdom brought through frequently costly experience acquired too late? Had such vast and heterogeneous innovations been carried out by the local and foreign participants in a process which carried the double standard of political emancipation and mercantile liberalization as far as to render Spanish America too unstable to regain equilibrium, even at the price of stagnation? It has already been seen that, in strictly economic terms, the answer

[51] Miers, *Travels,* II: 382–385.

must be conditional and not necessarily pessimistic. The fact that contemporary observers were inclined to be downhearted about the results of this process was due, at least in part, to the indirect economic consequences of these innovations, and even more to the cultural and political changes which took place contemporaneously and which affected the whole Spanish American way of life. This circumstance added further complications to an already highly complex situation and gave weight to the dominant feeling of uncertainty as to the future of Spanish America after 1825.

3

THE IMPACT OF THE OUTSIDE WORLD
ON SPANISH AMERICAN LIFE

Although less general than could have been expected, the economic innovations which took place contemporaneously with commercial liberalization had enormous consequences on Spanish American life, not only because they were based on altered consumption patterns, which were bound to affect every aspect of everyday life, but because they contributed to hasten a crisis among the prerevolutionary urban elite already hit by the changes which revolution had wrought in the political power structure.

It soon became apparent that revolution did not merely imply replacement of the predominantly Spanish career dignitaries with the sons of the Creole urban elite and that these positions would not necessarily retain their former prestige and power. For that elite sector of society, then, the economic situation confirmed and aggravated the disruption of the political order. The new freedom of trade not only reduced the former privileges of the wealthy merchants in the larger trading centers but brought rivals who held as their trump card the fact that they were the emissaries of the new metropolitan economy, Britain.

The leading sectors of the former colonial society were thus not only in a general state of crisis arising out of the revolution. They were also about to undergo the consequences of increasing contact with the outside world, which would be particularly painful because the exemplary success of the British merchants was attributed not only to their economic strength but to a general all-encompassing superiority.

It was not indeed their economic success which enabled the British traders to command the respect demanded by the powerful nation which jealously defended them and which caused them to be feared so reverentially that, in the midst of wars and persecutions, they were serenely able to pursue their way of life in Spanish America and were only rarely disturbed. In the Río de la Plata area examples of such fear and respect extend over a fifty-year period. During the ten years following the revolution, the Robertson brothers profited enormously from trafficking between Buenos Aires and the area held by Artigas, the separatist leader of the Littorine provinces, which no citizen of Buenos Aires could have attempted. Ten years later, in the midst of the Brazilian conflict, the same Robertson brothers used their official commission for carrying newly minted copper coin from Buenos Aires to the provincial army stationed on the banks of the Uruguay River to organize a pleasure trip with some of their fellow countrymen. After visiting the camp of the Buenos Aires troops, the jolly company was detained for several hours by the Brazilians, and so shocked at the insolence of this decision that, with diplomatic assistance, it saw to it that the officers responsible for it were exemplarily punished. Nearly twenty years later, while the respective governments of Buenos Aires and Montevideo were at war with each other, in Buenos Aires the Mazorca, the association of General Rosas's terrorist supporters, was patriotically collecting funds for the campaign with understandable success. But while the partisans and even the secret adversaries of the Rosas regime were rivaling each other in the generosity of their donations, a group of English traders refused to contribute at all. Their reasons were nothing but frank: they stated that since they dealt with Montevideo as well as with Buenos Aires they were disinclined to meet the reproaches of the governor of Montevideo, their good friend General Rivera, for subsidizing his enemy. This episode has been recorded not because of the reprisals which followed it but rather because of the apparently successful negotiations of the local representative of His Majesty's Government, who prevented the collection agents from continuing to importune the British merchants. After the fall of Rosas in 1852 when Buenos Aires was under siege by the provincial troops and it became difficult to bury the city's dead because the cemetery lay outside the enemy lines, a group of English residents obtained authorization from both sides to cross them whenever they wished to play cricket in the nearby countryside.[1]

Economic success was thus not the only factor which made the British almost the representatives of a different species of humanity from the ordinary mortals who were spared none of the hardships of the times. The very frequency with which their superiority was evinced rendered irrelevant the resentment it provoked among the local inhabitants. As the British minister in Buenos Aires wrote to London in 1832, the fact that Rosas, who had no particular affection for foreigners and who made political use of popular animosity toward non-Catholics, should himself have donated the land on which the first Anglican church in Buenos Aires was built is additional proof that Britain's power was sufficient to make her subjects in Spanish America independent of the good will of those who successively controlled the local governments.

The indirect consequences of the changing relationship to the outside world thus appear to have been more widespread the greater the distance from the economic area in which change originated. But even in this area the awareness of change was greater than change itself. Productivity, for instance, improved but little, and even where it achieved a certain importance, it was not accompanied by economically significant modernization of techniques. The modern weaving factories of Puebla, the chocolate mill with hydraulic machinery imported from England which bore pleasant witness to the progress of civilization in Arequipa,[2] and that "well-equipped brewery" in the district of Chumba, Santiago de Chile,[3] were thus isolated instances of technical advances far more important to the observers of the time than to the Spanish American economy as a whole.

---

[1] Note from W. Parish Robertson to Consul Parish, Dec. 15, 1825, Public Record Office, London, F. O. 6/9, folio 43 et seq.; Mandeville (British representative in Buenos Aires) to Aberdeen, April 23, 1842, No. 32; F.O. 6/83, folio 202 et seq.; T. Woodbine Hinchcliff, *Viaje al Plata en 1861* (Buenos Aires, 1955), p. 45.

[2] F. Tristán, *Peregrinaciones* (Santiago de Chile, 1941), p. 187.

[3] M. Graham, *Diario* (Madrid, 1916), p. 269.

In the same way, the development of new means of transport was followed with passionate curiosity far out of proportion with its immediate impact on the economy. The introduction of steamships, which until 1840 had no significant effect on it, was regarded as a notable feature of modernization as much as twenty years earlier. María Graham could not easily forget that on July 7, 1822, she had sailed on the *Rising Star,* the first steamship to leave from a South American Pacific port.[4] A few years later the excited and inquisitive citizens of Buenos Aires were taking daily trips on the new steam vessels to the nearby village of San Fernando which, incidentally, was linked to the former by excellent land communications.

As previously stated, however, the aspect of economic change which most directly affected daily life was the change in consumption patterns. True, some of these changes are difficult to perceive. For example, only careful scrutiny of the hospital records brings to light the gradual substitution of English coal for local fuel. But in the majority of cases change was obvious, almost blatantly so, and the isolated examples of technical advances referred to earlier were often the result of a generalized attitudinal change on the part of the consumer. A particularly clear example is to be found in the altered use of cloth and clothing, which accounted in such large measure for the increased imports. True, this increase was due not only to the changing attitude on the part of the consumer but also to the great effort made by the British factories (with varying degrees of success) to imitate traditional goods such as the sarapes of Saltillo and the Río de la Plata ponchos.[5]

Even so, in the towns, and not among the upper classes alone, the expansion of imports ran a course parallel to a revolutionary concept of dress. The new and distinctive feature was not so much European fashion as fashion itself. In describing the dress of the ladies of Buenos Aires in the colonial period, Mariquita Sánchez felt no need to include a date. Year after year materials, color, and cut were the same, and although the situation had begun to change

---

[4] *Ibid.,* p. 220.
[5] H. G. Ward, *Mexico in 1827,* I (London, 1828): 313.

somewhat prior to 1810, as reflected, for instance, in the growth of imports of semiluxury German fabrics, really significant changes took place only later. According to Ward the change by means of which "European fashions had entirely taken place of those glaring colors, by which but too many of the prettiest women were disfigured," took place in Mexico between 1824 and 1827.[6] From Mexico to Buenos Aires women began enthusiastically to accept the new dictates of fashion which not only took for granted the acceptance of a new style, but above all that of periodically changing styles, which increased the consumption of imported cloth. The process was not restricted exclusively to the upper classes. In a society which ever since colonial times had been divided into only two sectors according to criteria which were not exclusively economic, any woman who did not wish to be associated with the lowest stratum had to use her ingenuity to follow the changing moods of fashion. True, local inventiveness very soon introduced capricious variants to the transatlantic model.

In Mexico, as Fanny Calderón mockingly noted, ladies' morning dresses were covered in diamonds;[7] in Buenos Aires, where precious stones were scarce, the adoption of Spanish combs of increasingly outrageous size was grist to the caricaturists; whatever the local variations, at no time did the emancipation of local taste indicate a return to the monotony of colonial times. Even men's wear was included in the revolution of fashion and led "the tailor's [to] become one of the best trades in the capital" in Santiago, Chile.[8]

The altered patterns of consumption also affected furniture and interior decoration. In dwelling on the primitive rusticity of a country house on the outskirts of Buenos Aires, the poet Esteban Echeverría refers to the protagonist of one of his epics as being seated "in the corridor of his rambling house on a large old armchair of the pre-May [1810] style," i.e., the colonial style.[9] Even

[6] *Ibid.,* II: 403.

[7] F. Calderón de la Barca, *Life in Mexico* (London, n.d.), p. 96.

[8] J. Miers, *Travels,* II (London, 1826): 238.

[9] E. Echeverría, *Obras* I (Buenos Aires, 1875): 190.

if most traditional buildings ran as yet little risk of being replaced by "substantial houses built of stone . . . of two or three stories in height," yet great effort was spent in decorating the old houses after the latest style.[10] While it is true that in Buenos Aires the Inquisition was already expressing alarm as early as 1796 over the modish use of imported wallpaper with an abundance of mythological motifs, a general trend became possible only when commercial freedom made imports from Europe more accessible.[11] Modernity was taken to signify, above all, ornate abundance. The most serious complaint lodged against the old style was its preference for stark austerity, regarded, not always erroneously, as a sign of collective penury. This new decorative ideal gave rise to interiors such as that of Doña Mercedes Rosales de Del Solar, in Santiago, Chile, "with a majestic French bed, open piano, guitar, ostentatious bronze clock . . . books, sewing materials, porcelain vases full of flowers."[12] Here, among purely decorative innovations, are others which point to a more profound change in the general way of life. Among these perhaps none was more significant than the profusion in which timepieces came to be used, sometimes as furnishings, sometimes as a complement to the dress of fashionable ladies and gentlemen. This new addition to timepieces had a fairly palpable effect on import statistics and allowed certain immigrant artisans to prosper, but it would be too much to say that it caused an overly rapid development of a sense of time and its use. The acquisition of this luxury item was restricted to a reduced sector of the urban population, and even in 1832 in the girls' schools of villages near Buenos Aires the scarcity of clocks was a problem. According to records of the period, in San Fernando "a clock is lacking, indispensable for the classes," and in Luján, a bit farther from Buenos Aires, "a pocket watch has been acquired, as it is easier to transport [than a clock to Buenos

[10] T. Sutchliffe, *Sixteen Years in Chile and Peru* (London, 1841), p. 161.
[11] José Toribio Medina, *La inquisición en el Río de la Plata* (Buenos Aires, 1945), p. 265.
[12] Graham, *Diario,* p. 264.

Aires] should it require repair, for there are no watchmakers there."[13]

Even less indicative of any real change in the way of life was the profusion of pianos, which eventually took up a more conspicuous place than the clock in the dowries of the wealthier and more fashion-conscious groups. Topography was a principal limiting factor in the piano addiction. In Popayán, isolated in the midst of the mountains, the brother of a rich merchant was proud of possessing the only piano in the district, which had cost him 1,200 pesos and had to be taken "from England to Guayaquil, and then in a small coaster to Buenaventura, whence it had been carried on the back of Negroes over the mountains to Popayán,"[14] but in Buenos Aires, Valparaíso, and Caracas, Broadwood pianos were more easily come by. Young ladies played them by ear to the appreciation or otherwise of their captive audience. While María Graham thought the Chilean girls played "with dexterity and taste," it is hardly surprising that the ill-humored Miers found the style of these improvisers detestable.[15]

The change to new uses extended far beyond dress and furniture. Martínez Sáenz, who traded on the Paraná, never forgot to take a good stock of English beer from Buenos Aires to Corrientes; it was far more efficacious than bribery in attenuating the severity of the customs house employees of Corrientes, and his guests held this drink in greater esteem than "chilled champagne in full summer" would have been held in Britain.[16] It was not only in provincial Corrientes that this beverage, in England most enthusiastically consumed below stairs, was considered a luxury: in the belief that inclination for beer was an aristocratic weakness, the minister of finances of Colombia, Castillo y Rada, proudly flaunted it.[17] But while the preference for imported beer rather

[13] Report from M. Sánchez, president of the Sociedad de Beneficencia, in Archivo General de la Nación (Buenos Aires), X, 6–1–5, cited by Evaristo Iglesias in *La escuela pública bonaerense hasta la caída de Rosas* (Buenos Aires, 1946), p. 235.

[14] J. P. Hamilton, *Travels,* II (London, 1827): 76.

[15] Graham, *Diario,* p. 173; Miers, *Travels,* II: 236.

[16] J. P. Robertson and G. P. Robertson, *Cartas de Sud-América,* I (Buenos Aires, 1950): 138.

[17] Hamilton, *Travels,* I: 173.

than local liquor certainly contributed to the extraordinary growth of imports, it is again doubtful that it could have implied a profound modernization of the way of life. What is evident is the relationship between these innovations, in which the concept was frequently more important than the substance, and the deliberate tendency toward modernization. What attracted the consumers to English beer was not the dubious pleasure of a drink which can hardly have been improved by long and hazardous journeying over tropical seas, but the fact that to drink it was above all an implicit act of faith in the superiority of that which was foreign and modern over that which was traditional and local.

This opening toward the outside world which underlay the transformation of the consumption patterns was also apparent in changes which were only partially related to it. In Arequipa, around 1840, French dances took the place of the local ones, which were "considered reprehensible" according to the unexpectedly puritanical Flora Tristán, "for reasons of decency." Almost twenty years earlier, in "one of the most out of the way and least frequented spots in the civilized world," according to Basil Hall's unflattering description of Payta in northern Peru, the traveler heard a native harpist play "with considerable spirit a waltz which not very long before, *he* had heard as a fashionable air in London."[18] And even in more recondite places travelers found signs of this growing openness toward the outside world. In Guatavita, an Indian village in Nueva Granada, the living room of the village priest's house was adorned somewhat incongruously with the portrait of George II of England.[19]

Modernization thus proved to be a process richer in symbolic content than in any material change in everyday living, although its shortcomings in the latter respect must not be exaggerated, since even the most primitive areas underwent a deep process of transformation once exposed to commercial contact with the foreigner over a period of time. No area, for instance, could have been further removed from what passed for a civilized way of life than the cattle-raising pampas of Buenos Aires. Travelers crossing it ten

---

[18] B. Hall, *Extracts from a Journal,* II (Edinburgh, 1824): 77.
[19] Hamilton, *Travels,* I: 190.

or fifteen years after the revolution never tired of describing its unbelievably primitive aspect. Miers stresses his astonishment on seeing "clothes hanging out to dry" near Rojas, less than twenty leagues from Buenos Aires.[20] Ten years later in the midst of a holy war against his political enemies, whose party color was blue, Juan Manuel de Rosas found it necessary to warn the rural police of the astuteness of the perfidious enemy who had taken advantage of rustic innocence. Throughout the countryside women were washing with a new product which, under pretext of whitening clothes more efficiently, left them with a decidedly bluish tinge. It would seem, from this observation, that the custom of washing clothes not only with primitive tallow soaps but with additives of a certain sophistication had spread within ten years to the backward countryside.

In due course—especially in those areas best integrated to the new economy—the process of modernization would appear to have been less superficial than impatient witnesses held it to have been in 1825. To its protagonists, however, it was primarily the shortcomings of the process which were apparent. While they were not always aware to what extent the effects of modernization were concentrated within a limited social sector, they did clearly perceive that it was not easy to adapt to modernity without incongruence. Thus, while the elegant of Buenos Aires, Santiago, and Lima rode in coaches of irreproachable European manufacture, travelers who disembarked in Buenos Aires or Valparaíso had occasion both to see and to use carts so primitively built that no metal was used in their construction.[21] Furthermore, exposure to the new economic order made people aware of new methods and new technology, but it did not always provide the necessary materials in abundance.[22] In the Río de la Plata area, in 1829 the governor of the relatively isolated province of Santiago del Estero was obliged to warn his correspondent, the head of a military regime in Córdoba, that he would shortly be obliged to interrupt his correspon-

[20] Miers, *Travels,* I: 31.
[21] Tristán, *Peregrinaciones,* p. 295.
[22] Miers, *Travels,* I: 3; Graham, *Diario,* p. 163.

dence because he was gradually losing his sharpness of sight and was unable to find a pair of spectacles anywhere in the province under his government; he hoped that his Córdoba correspondent might perhaps be fortunate enough to find him a pair. But even in Valparaíso, center of overseas trade for the whole of Chile, the governor was to confess that the market could not provide him with a coffee grinder for his own personal use.[23]

This was but an added reason why modernizing endeavors concentrated in those areas where a necessarily limited material transformation would produce results richest in symbolic content. Such a trend could only accentuate the tension between concept and value systems which modernization had brought in its wake and the physical context which it was able to modify only very slightly. To be sure, it was not so much the tension which was new as the terms on which it now existed. Long before its partial adaptation to the new postrevolutionary ideals, Spanish America had undergone an equally approximative adaptation to those of the prerevolutionary period. The hypocrisies and ambiguities, which were no longer even perceived as such, were nothing new in that region which was not then making its first attempt to live in accordance with a code of juridical, social, and cultural norms evolved in an alien context. As in the colonial period and perhaps to a greater extent than formerly, political activities continued to show a tendency to accentuate the incongruity between Spanish America as it was and the ideals with which it tried to identify itself. Financial penury was here the decisive factor. Even those regimes most decidedly set on radical innovation could devote to it only the most meager sums. Since canals, roads, and ports were so costly, the desire to innovate could be demonstrated in a manner equally ostentatious and far less burdensome by surrounding a strip of land with a wall and thus creating a "pantheon" which, for lack of other centers of attraction close to the city, finally became

[23] Felipe Ibarra to J. M. Paz, Santiago, May 12, 1829, in Alfredo Gargaro, *Paz e Ibarra* (Santiago del Estero, 1942), p. 55; Diego Portales to A. Garfias, April 4, 1832, in *Epistolario de Diego Portales,* II (Santiago de Chile, 1936): 156.

(in Arequipa, Santiago de Chile, and Buenos Aires) the Mecca of travelers and local sightseers. In spite of its neoclassical-sounding name, the pantheon was a cemetery, a piece of consecrated land in which no dissident could be interred. Even so, the creation of the so-called pantheons, which was followed closely by abolition of the custom of burial within the church, traditionally considered the Christian burial *par excellence,* could not but affect the place of religion and the Church in society. This indirect effect was the more clearly apparent because many, like the Argentine Sarmiento (who on visiting the pantheon of Valparaíso enthusiastically referred to it as "that beautiful garden full of pyramidal pilasters to which families come for a stroll") attributed the innovation to Protestant influence.[24] Consequently, where the creation of a pantheon was not complemented by prohibition of burial in church on the grounds that it was prejudicial to public health, only those who could not afford a church burial ended up in the pantheon, which rapidly became the neglected cemetery of the poor, as was the case in Santiago.[25] When, on the other hand, this prohibition was imposed, it roused considerable protest, particularly among the more important families who feared to lose that posthumous recognition of their eminence which the meticulously hierarchical distribution of places of burial within the church had ensured them in the past, and lost no opportunity of presenting their snobbish fears as religious scruples.

Penury was not always responsible for such reforms, which were so limited in comparison to the controversies they triggered. In the 1820s and in more than one Spanish American area, a very generalized interest in the propagation of instruction brought about the creation of schools based on the Lancasterian system, which allowed maximum utilization of the reduced financial and human resources of the new states. The process was by no means superficial. In Nueva Granada, John Hamilton was surpised to find, on his "travels to the south and westward, a school on the Lan-

---

24 D. F. Sarmiento, "Un viaje a Valparaíso," in *Obras completas,* I (Buenos Aires, 1948): 138.

25 Miers, *Travels,* II: 260.

casterian system in every village," and in Buenos Aires the new method allowed a comparable expansion of the network of primary country schools.[26] But in the long run the system broke down, and at less elementary levels modernization of teaching methods soon provoked controversy. A penchant for the most modern and prestigious doctrines still adhered to in Europe by the so-called liberal-constitutionalists in the midst of the Restoration, which Spanish America accepted in a modified form, was suddenly found to be incompatible with that adherence to a religious faith which had provided the core for prerevolutionary cultural tradition. The drive toward educational innovation received no definite support from economically powerful groups, which could not expect to obtain tangible and immediate benefits from it, and it became yet another cause of increased tension.

Such reforms as poverty permitted, by stressing cultural and even ideological factors, increasingly fragmented the generalized effort toward innovation. On a long-term basis even their low material cost—in the midst of political situations of still questionable stability—was too high for the possibilities of the meager state budgets. As has been hinted, reducing their target to those areas in which a minimum material transformation achieved a maximum symbolic implication of the change wrought by independence on the collective beliefs and attitudes of the community, the postrevolutionary states continued to follow, in their own way, a tendency already deeply rooted in prerevolutionary Spanish America. Altered circumstances, however, profoundly affected the significance of this tendency. While colonial Spanish America had been ill-suited to the complex of principles and convictions which constituted the basis of its form of government, at least these principles and convictions were not seriously disputed. The revolutionary governments, on the other hand, had to contend with the heritage of a colonial past which, although initially rejected, was viewed with increasing indulgence as time went by and at worst criticized only from a political angle. They thus faced a less malleable situation than they had optimistically anticipated, and

26 Hamilton, *Travels,* I: 253.

their so modest reformist ambitions aroused the hostility of large sectors still loyal to a system of values toward which even the reformist rulers displayed an increasingly nostalgic affection. The most powerful force identifying with this far from dead tradition was the Church, an institution which could not be overlooked. It is hardly surprising that its status should have been one of the causes of dispute regarding the consequences of postrevolutionary modernization in Spanish America.

The altered commercial situation, as already noted, gave to a foreign and heretical group a dominant and unshakable position in the economy of the new nations, making a clash with the prerevolutionary concept of unity of faith as inevitable as insoluble. The clergy who exalted "amiable political freedom" from the pulpit while railing against those who, as a legitimate corollary, upheld "freedom of conscience" were probably sincere in doing so.[27] But, while not necessarily a corollary of political freedom, a certain degree of religious tolerance appeared to be the inevitable consequence of commercial liberalization. The question of religious tolerance became so urgent because it posed implicitly the whole set of problems which the statute of the Church created. Some of these problems derived from the political sphere itself. It was the loyalty to the ecclesiastical policy of the Spanish Crown, rather than the tendency to a new and revolutionary one, which made the problem more acute.

In the colonial period the Church had been firmly subjected to government control. The inability of the latter to exercise this control in outlying areas frequently limited its practical consequences, but in no wise denied the validity of the principle. The independence wars had only accentuated this dependence. It has already been seen that the takeover of political power by one or another faction was responsible for the impoverishment of the Church and a reduction of its privileges (and, as N. Farriss has pointed out in the case of Mexico, the royalist party was more

---

[27] Sermon of Fray Luis Pacheco, Catamarca, May 25, 1817, in *El Clero Argentino,* I (Buenos Aires, 1911): 224.

ruthless than the Revolutionary in this respect).[28] These inroads met with only sporadic and formal protest from the clergy, themselves too deeply committed to the struggle to argue with the heads of the parties with which they had eventually sided. Once the wars of independence were over, the postrevolutionary governments wished to maintain their power over the Church, further consolidated by war, and to use this power to impose upon it a series of reforms which, although vast, affected only its organization. This attempt provoked violent and briefly successful reactions.

Ecclesiastical reform was indeed one of the main subjects of political debate during the 1820s. These reforms covered a vast area. It was, in the first place, the situation of the religious orders themselves which attracted the attention of the reformers. Hostility was not essentially new. Even without taking into account criticisms current since the late Middle Ages of the sort of piety practiced in the convent, the Enlightenment had begun to judge them from an economic and social point of view and to conclude that the benefits which the religious orders offered to society as a whole were not proportionate to the riches which they controlled. This conclusion was based on the implicit but very decided adoption of a worldly system of values which rejected the validity of a life directed toward contemplation, or works aimed at the spiritual salvation of the individual rather than at social welfare. In accordance with this attitude the reformers sought on the one hand to make it more difficult for the religious orders to increase their wealth and on the other to discourage people from joining them. The same hostility was manifest also in enforcing with renewed vigor the laws ruling the maximum and minimum number of secular members permitted to each convent for the purpose— sometimes openly admitted—of abolishing as many convents as possible.

The attitude toward the secular clergy was more favorable. The same enlightened authors who rejected the idea of withdrawal from the world as expounded by the religious orders saw in the

---

[28] N. Farriss, *Crown and Clergy in Colonial Mexico, 1759–1821: The Crisis of Ecclesiastical Privilege* (London, 1968), chap. 9.

parish priests the most suitable instrument for propagating the new ideas, at that juncture still the preserve of a minority, among vast sectors of the population. They decided that the secular clergy would be the best instrument to guide the faithful toward both eternal salvation and earthly wealth and felicity. Thus, the Bourbon monarchy made use of the pulpit to broadcast the recently rediscovered technique of the Caesarian section, and, in a less episodic fashion, of vaccination. An engraving which circulated from Guatemala to Buenos Aires characteristically celebrated the two aspects, profane and sacred, of the secular clergy's mission. It depicts a priest holding up with veneration an object surrounded by the halo which imagery usually reserved for the sacrament carried to the dying. The man wielding it, however, is not proposing to assist at a Christian death. He is carrying the vaccination lancet, instrument of a secular and constantly repeated miracle, which will save the entire Spanish Indies from a terrible scourge.

During the revolution, advantage was taken of the possibility of finding new, secular, and, more immediately, political use for the prestige of the parish priests. This fact served to confirm their right to a position within the postrevolutionary order. To be sure, the precise position which they were to occupy continued to be the cause of some dispute, but this dispute centered in still comparatively benign controversies over the tithe. The harm wrought by the tithe on agriculture had been stressed—indeed exaggerated—ever since the eighteenth century. The fact that the civil authorities who collected it could retain a generally important percentage of the funds collected weakened the arguments of those in favor of its suppression. The arguments against the tithe drew strength from the support of the landowning groups who frequently managed to obtain reductions of the tithe or even temporary exemptions, on the grounds that they were promoting certain forms of agriculture undergoing particularly bad times. The final abolition of the tithe did not take long, and caused even less acute conflicts than might have been expected from the frequently lively discussions which preceded it. This was due primarily to the reputation which the tribute had acquired in Spanish America: not only did the civil authority, as mentioned above, retain a part of the income derived from the tithe, but the most extreme regalists considered the state its rightful recipient. Thus José A. de San Alberto, bishop of Córdoba and subsequently archbishop of Charcas, attributed the transference of a fraction of the revenue from the tithe to generosity rather than obligation on the part of the state.[29] In fact, although in principle abolition of the tithe was disadvantageous to the Church, it did not imply any radical reform of its legal position. Furthermore, the substitution of the uncertain income derived from the tithe, frequently difficult to collect in outlying districts, with a direct subsidy from the state by no means always signified a reduction of the sum actually received by the Church.

Reforms affecting the secular and regular clergy in postrevolutionary times had one element in common: in them disputes over Church wealth after the Revolution were not as important as they were to be in the wave of secularization which took place in much of Spanish America during the second half of the century. To what was this due? On the one hand, the treasures of the Church and its orders had been greatly affected during the course of the wars by destruction and enforced contributions, and thus, in the postrevolutionary period, these resources were less frequently resorted to and their use could no longer be regarded as a scandalous innovation. Insofar as the Church's real estate was concerned (and in some countries this was more than considerable), the very state of economic stagnation which during that period stabilized the situation of the lands of the Indians perhaps protected the ecclesiastic lands from the greed of those who wished to gain or to increase their own. While this comparative indifference to the Church's worldly assets lessened tensions, it made the victory of the radical innovators more uncertain, since no socioeconomic power group felt its interests to be identified with them.

In other respects, changes imposed by the state to the position of the Church evoked still less controversy. Thus, in Lima and Buenos Aires the state or new lay associations were able to take without widespread scandal the place of the religious orders in hospital and welfare work. The innovation which caused, perhaps,

[29] J. A. de San Alberto, *Cartas pastorales* (Madrid, 1793), p. 97.

least resistance was the abolition of the Inquisition. It had roused almost universal ill feeling, shared even by the majority of those who regarded religious tolerance with horror. Naturally enough, its abolition did not put an end to the persecution of heretics. On the contrary, the function formerly restricted to the holy office was shared out among the ecclesiastical authorities (in charge of maintaining discipline not only among the clergy but also among the faithful) and the civil authorities who undertook the guard against impious literature. In fact, the suppression of the Inquisition did bring about a relaxation of the vigilance maintained over orthodoxy and discipline among the faithful without causing undue comment, and while in certain areas of Spanish America those accused of impiety, found the doors of their friends' homes and even of their furnishers closed to them, any more direct forms of punishment would have implied a resumption of the practices to which the Inquisition owed its deplorable notoriety and which were no longer found acceptable. But although even the most enthusiastic defenders of unity of faith would not abide dissenters' being treated as criminals, the attitude toward the propagation of heterodox books and ideas was another matter altogether, and in this point a far larger part of the population eyed indulgence with disfavor. The civil authorities responsible for this aspect of repression displayed an intermittent willingness to listen to their exigencies (and at times to use them to prevent the diffusion of politically unsuitable literature). Thus, in Buenos Aires at the beginning of the 1830s, books and other reading material were once again publicly burned, and toward the end of the following decade the entire edition of *Sociabilidad Chilena,* Francisco Bilbao's harsh indictment of the Catholic and Spanish tradition still dominant in Republican Chile, was solemnly burned by the executioner in Santiago. This form of repression was, however, as inefficient as it was strident. It is enough to read the advertisements which Buenos Aires booksellers published in the daily press to realize that not even the Rosas government—which was hardly lacking in tenacity—was disposed to struggle persistently against the "poison bound in gold paste" which the ecclesiastical papers denounced in vain. In Chile the Argentine Sarmiento, favored by the Conservative goverment which had ordered the burning of Bilbao's book, defended this measure with arguments which only prove to what extent the purifying zeal of the regime had cooled. The executioner, according to Sarmiento, had justly chastised the author for his clumsiness. What Bilbao stated had already been said in Chile by many writers, including Sarmiento himself, and the denunciations which made all of them out to be enemies of the traditional faith were disregarded by all persons of sense. Tact was indeed all that was required.

Thus circumstances created a new status for the Church and the Catholic faith. While their predominance was no longer ensured, they were protected against direct onslaught which could only too easily lead to pure insult. It was hard to provide any greater support than this, and the disputes concerning the curriculum taught by state institutions is revealing evidence of the fact. Although opposition to certain authors (Bentham in Nueva Granada, Condillac in the Río de la Plata) or certain teachers who too enthusiastically supported theories which clashed with points of religious dogma—negation of the soul's immortality, for instance —was eventually successful, success was essentially negative: while propagation of the more explicitly anti-Christian theories was halted, what was not achieved, and perhaps was never intended, was to impose upon education a coherently Christian and Catholic orientation. Twenty years after Juan Crisostomo Lafinur, as an impetuous admirer of Condillac, was forced to abandon both his teaching and the city of Buenos Aires itself, substantially similar ideas were being expounded with singular authority by Dr. Diego Alcorta, and neither the zealous government of Rosas nor the "idiotic bigots" who were supposed to have such strong influence over him saw in this any cause for concern.

The consequences of the traditionalist reaction in Spanish America should then not be exaggerated. It was more energetic than coherent. The region endeavored simultaneously to remain loyal to its religious tradition and to achieve the heights of enlightenment characteristic of the times. Although the religious tensions of the 1830s revealed the vitality of the traditionalist feelings in the community as a whole and drew attention to the political consequences born of ignoring them, those who made political use of the doctrine of Catholic integralism regarded it rather as an *instrumentum regni* than a doctrine worthy of taking into serious consideration. Characteristically, when in 1825 and 1826 the province of Córdoba, Argentina, staged a revolt against the National Congress which would not accept the reelection of the governor, the obdurate province unhesitatingly deployed against Congress all the most traditionally intolerant arguments of Catholicism. The very names of the daily papers founded specifically to propagate these arguments are themselves revealing (*The Intolerant, The Old Christian*). Curiously enough, while inciting to religious war, the Provincial Legislature relieved its members of the obligation to use a religious wording for the oath they offered when taking office. The reason given for this reform was that a religious oath could only be considered a relic of past superstition no longer tolerable in an enlightened age.[30] Thus the rulers of the province of Córdoba clung to the best of both worlds: steeped in traditional faith, they wished to be recognized also as men of their times. This peculiar dichotomy made unavoidable a certain flexibility in the attitudes of the political leaders. The religious problem was, in fact, political, and it was therefore natural that postures assumed with reference to religious questions should have the conditional and circumstantial character typical of politics. While the Conservatives of Nueva Granada found much to object to in the headlong career of General José María Obando, idol toward the end of the forties of an increasingly anticlerical Liberal party, they were displaying a strange indulgence toward the fact that ten years earlier he had headed a bigoted movement of protest against the abolition of certain convents in Pasto. His crusade had changed into a movement almost diametrically opposed to his original stated objectives without his losing either his followers or his political respectability (while the latter was certainly repudiated by his adversaries, this was for profoundly different reasons).

The institutional weakness of the Church contributed to the

---

[30] Ernesto A. Celesia, *El federalismo argentino: Córdoba,* III (Buenos Aires, 1932): 249.

ambiguity of its political role in the new nations. While plenty of the clergy upheld tradition in the strictest sense, their right to speak for the institution they defended was frequently no more clearly established than that of those members who happened to favor innovations. After centuries of obedience to the Crown, and more than ten years' association with impassioned political causes, the ecclesiastical structure had suffered heavy setbacks. There were numerous vacant bishoprics, administered by priests appointed by the civil authorities. The independence of the religious orders had been further restricted by the decision to annul their allegiance to their superiors in Spain and to place them instead under the aegis of the local bishop or even of authorities specially created by the governments for their supervision. These complex changes of fortune do not alone account for the reluctance of the dignitaries of the Spanish American Church to undertake crusades against modernity which could only have upset the close relationship which they had established with the local governments. The doctrinarian and cultural centers and the attraction which the more advanced cultural trends held for the more enlightened among them must also be taken into account.

Eventually the echo of the European Restoration was felt even in South America. It called for a brand of Catholicism less amenable to modernity, one which was able to adapt itself to the growing importance of the sectors which had become politically influential as a result of the French Revolution, by simultaneously affirming the authority of Rome and converting unshakable—if unenlightened—loyalty of the rural masses into the mainstay of the Church.

The echo was, however, weak and late in coming. In the first place, to have made its hegemony over the Spanish American Church most efficiently felt, Rome would have had to reestablish public contact with it and contribute to its prompt return to normality. While some Spanish American governments urged Rome to proceed, others regarded the prospect with alarm. None would have been able efficiently to prevent the Roman Curia, had it moved with decision, from reestablishing its supremacy over the Church of the Indies. But for the Holy See—in the context of

Catholic Europe hard at work restoring prerevolutionary regimes —there was an implicit risk involved in acknowledging situations which owed their very existence to the downfall of the old European order. Since the king of Spain, legitimate head of the Spanish Indies, would not relinquish his rights of patronage over its church, even direct appointment of bishops by the pope, without previously consulting the new civil authorities, would have carried the implication that the king no longer held the authority to appoint bishops. This obstacle impeded, but could not altogether prevent, the process of normalization from taking place. Already at the close of the 1820s the pope was allowing the investiture of new bishops in Gran Colombia and, disregarding the Spanish sovereign's right of patronage, accepting proposals made by the republican government in a manner suspiciously similar to that used by the king when those rights were undisputed. All in all, the situation was such that change had to take place discreetly. This being the case, the Roman Curia was not always able to take full advantage of it.

Within the structure of the Church itself, the advance of Rome on the periphery, which was based on plebeian piety, was bound to awaken strong resistance in Spanish America. The animosity of those who had become leaders of the local churches thanks to isolation and revolution was not only a result of fear of losing their authority, which they knew to be frail. Both regalist tradition— inherited from the best among the prelates of late colonial times— and modernist sympathies preferred them to judge without indulgence an enterprise which appeared to them to be politically dangerous and culturally unenlightened.

The cleric who administered the bishopric of Buenos Aires was not being merely servile in making common cause with the local governor and displaying hostility toward the mission sent by the Holy See to the Río de la Plata and Chile in 1824 to gather information and resume contact with the churches which had been cut off for so long. In taking such a stand he was being loyal to tendencies which were manifest also in the liberality which the ecclesiastical authorities displayed in granting licenses for mixed marriages. These same proclivities later led some of Rosas's more zealous advisers to propose transferring the authority to concede such dispensations to the civil authorities, who would be more likely to maintain the former strict injunctions with regard to heretics.

It is equally unsurprising that political leaders should have adopted an attitude similar to that of the ecclesiastical innovators. A Catholic renaissance, in the form of a direct appeal to the reserves of traditional devotion of the masses, over the heads of the political and ecclesiastical leaders, was unlikely to appeal to them. It threatened to reduce their authority, and since Spanish American political leaders were not prepared to accept the difficulties created by political mobilization, however circumscribed, they were bound to regard without indulgence a movement which was bent on increasing the power of an entity independent of the local political apparatus, although prepared to make political use of the misoneism of wide sectors of public opinion.

Political leaders were even less inclined to accept intolerance toward foreign dissenters, although it was certainly widespread even in those sectors of Spanish America in which tolerance was practiced, and without giving rise to unpleasant incidents. De facto respect for the freedom of the dissenters was displayed as much by the rulers who kept their distance from traditional Catholicism, as by those who fervently proclaimed their devotion. The extent to which Rosas thought fit to display good will toward the Anglican (and subsequently the Presbyterian) church of Buenos Aires has already been mentioned. The fact that the dissenters occupied a position within the new economy which made them simultaneously feared, hated, and envied added a new and perhaps decisive dimension to the dilemma.

Present-day historians who feel deep sympathy toward the governments who tried to halt the advance of foreign economic dominance but are unable to identify themselves with the slogan "religion or death" hasten to point out that sometimes the defense of religious faith takes the place of a "national defensive ideology." This interpretation oversimplifies an essentially ambiguous stance. For example, the legislature of the Argentine province of Tucumán simultaneously refused to approve the treaty with Great

Britain authorizing the practice of the dissenting faith and revealed lively interest in reaching an agreement with Captain Joseph Andrews, "commissioned by a Company formed in London to work mines in South America," concerning exploitation of the hypothetical mines which might be found in the province.[31] Furthermore, precisely because a resistance of tolerating the dissenting faith was frequently associated with the opposition to the new commercial connection, the former proved to be of negligible political efficacy, except as a slogan with which to rouse the populace, conveniently forgotten once victory had been achieved. In fact, only those who stood to gain from a crisis in the relationship with the new economic metropolis proposed intolerance as a practicable policy and not merely as a demagogical resource. As that relationship was consolidated, those prejudiced thereby underwent the irreversible consequences of progressive economic deterioration. Consequently their political influence became increasingly limited. Those who were aware that their prosperity depended upon the presence of those unwelcome guests (however much they might abhor all that which was foreign and heretical) became more and more influential. Chile was not the only country to which the maliciously lucid observation of Miers could be applied, stating that "notwithstanding the violent prejudices against foreigners . . . the circumstances of the times have now made it impossible to exclude them, since the chief resource and revenue of the state, as well as the trade and income of the aristocratical community itself, must greatly depend on the foreign trade, which has become necessary to its support."[32]

It was not, however, only self-interest which accounted for this good will. The attitude of the Spanish American elite toward the emissaries of the new merchant metropolis was not characterized throughout by the incontestable predominance of "violent prejudices." On the contrary, it was based rather on a very generalized prejudice in their favor, which only gradually yielded to disillu-

---

[31] Rodolfo Ortega Peña and Eduardo Luis Duhalde, *Facundo y la montonera* (Buenos Aires, 1968), pp. 116, 313–319.

[32] Miers, *Travels,* II: 141–142.

sionment and was at no time conspicuous for its systematic hostility. Even the clergy themselves adopted this attitude. In still-Spanish Lima the archbishop expounded on the vehemence of his Anglophile sentiments to Basil Hall, exalting the advantages of freedom of trade and other civil rights, and although such extravagant terms can only have been partially sincere, they revealed at least a positive wish to live without conflict with these new members of society.[33] In Nueva Granada, the future archbishop, Joaquín Mosquera, showed all the signs of the Anglomania which momentarily possessed the Creole elite, imitating the habits and customs of the English as far as he was able.[34]

True, the idea of peaceful coexistence with the heretic awoke the indignation of some. In Chile Miers accused the clergy of inciting "the more fanatical and lower classes against foreigners";[35] in Nueva Granada, Hamilton himself described the fiery oratory of the priest of Fucutativá, whose tirade against foreigners included them as "Jews and Heretics."[36] But these episodes serve to show that the alliance of the religious conservatives and hostile populace against a new order characterized by the ascendancy of non-Catholic foreigners weakened rather than strengthened the forces of reaction. In Chile the government ran no risk in ignoring the appeals to xenophobia. In Nueva Granada, in the incident cited by Hamilton, the civil authorities brought the too eloquent priest of Fucutativá to trial by an ecclesiastical tribunal which deprived him of his living and imposed a fine on him.

The intolerance of the populace was not the only threat to peaceful coexistence with the dissenters, which became increasingly difficult as the newcomers took to proselytizing or too ostentatiously refrained from paying deference to the established faith, thus drawing attention to themselves and cruelly stressing the fact that religious unanimity had ended. While the funeral processions of the dissenters crossed the streets of the cities of Spanish

---

[33] Hall, *Journal,* I: 94.
[34] Hamilton, *Travels,* II: 34.
[35] Miers, *Travels,* II: 223.
[36] Hamilton, *Tarvels,* I: 258.

America in broad daylight, causing no scandal of any sort, and were eventually attended even by Catholic priests, the refusal of the dissenters to pay due respect to the sacrament when it was being carried to the dying gave rise to incidents everywhere from Caracas to Buenos Aires.

An elaborate system of meticulous reciprocal courtesy was thus established. The openly acknowledged dissenters took part in Catholic celebrations. María Graham did so in Buenos Aires. In the port of San Blas on the Mexican Pacific, where Basil Hall found greater concern over religious questions than anywhere else in Spanish America, and where he was asked more frequently than elsewhere whether he was Catholic, his negative reply provoked no revulsion among his hearers. Even there "they . . . always considered our regular attendance at mass and other attentions to their customs as marks of civility and good will." This display of courtesy was frequently spontaneous and a sign of reciprocal good will. Quite apart from any programmed support of the principle of religious tolerance, more than one village priest appears enthusiastically to have received the visit of a traveling English dissenter whose arrival cheered the monotony of his daily existence. From the frontiers of Quito to Bogotá Hamilton had excellent recollections of the hospitality of the clergy, on whom he depended constantly. At times, too, this cordial relationship had a more permanent basis. When in Buenos Aires, María Graham attended mass with her friend Mrs. Campbell; Spanish dress and mantilla being considered *de rigueur* in church, both ladies, to their considerable vexation, had to change out of their elegant French clothes and hats. Contrary to what might have been the initial impression of the absent-minded reader, Mrs. Campbell was not a compatriot of Mrs. Graham, but a Creole and the sister of the preacher whom both were going to hear.[37]

By means of such contrivances the dissenters managed to avoid the danger of being outcast by local society because of their religious peculiarities. Obviously, the economic advantages of tolerance were very clear and the tactics employed to avoid segregation

[37] Hall, *Journal,* II: 235; Graham, *Diario,* p. 192.

by no means novel. At the beginning of the eighteenth century, when the agents of a British company which had a monopoly on the import of Negroes set up a subsidiary in Buenos Aires, as a consequence of the Treaty of Utrecht, they became very friendly with the local Jesuits, from whom they received credit and to whom they gave generous donations. They thus simultaneously established useful contacts with the local economy and gained protection from any local reaction against their heretical presence.[38] There were other reasons also why at that particular juncture, at the beginning of the nineteenth century, still characterized by the series of wars throughout which Great Britain encouraged and successfully supported the European counterrevolution, English hostility toward Catholicism, which had played a significant role throughout, should have abated. While travelers continued to remark upon the misdemeanors of the clergy, these were very frequently attributed not so much to the nature of the Church itself as to the general crisis of moral standards in revolutionary Spanish America. Comparing the Jesuits with the secular clergy and the religious orders whose shortcomings were only too apparent, British travelers frequently praised the former and decried their expulsion.[39]

The postrevolutionary period paved the way for collaboration in the specifically religious domain by revealing the advance of irreligion as a danger common to all sects. True, with the recuperating Roman See in the throes of reorganization, the character of Catholicism at that juncture scarcely lent itself to such experiment. Even so, the efforts of the Bible Society to propagate holy texts met with very different reactions in Colombia under Santander than in Spain under Ferdinand VII. And while it is also true that the prelates who initially protected it eventually stopped doing so, the very fact that during a not inconsiderable period of time important local ecclesiastics and the non-Catholic agents of a non-Catholic society were able jointly to participate in a pious

---

[38] G. Furlong, *Thomas Falkner y su "Acerca de los patagones"* (Buenos Aires, 1949), pp. 12–14.

[39] A. Caldcleugh, *Travels in South America,* I (London, 1825): 185.

undertaking stresses the peculiar character of the religious temper of postrevolutionary Spanish America.

Would it be true to state that in postrevolutionary Spanish America the only role of the dissenter was to accord welcome support to Catholicism in resisting the onslaughts of impiety? This was not precisely the case. While celebrating the end of the "reign of bigotry," Hamilton deplored the frequency with which public opinion swung from one extreme to the other, "having little or no religion; their minds being poisoned by reading the works of Voltaire, Jean Jacques Rousseau and other free thinkers."[40] But, however discreetly the colonial status of Catholicism was discarded (and it must be recalled that Catholicism had not only been the religion of the state and the community, explicitly or implicitly part of each collective action or individual decision, but also by definition the unanimous faith of the whole Spanish American continent), this abandon was bound to offer a very strong justification to those who did not want to exclude religion from their effort to break the continuity of the prerevolutionary past. The Church was particularly vulnerable to this sort of criticism because, even if ready enough unobtrusively to revise its conduct, it could not bring itself publicly to abandon the rigidly held bastions of the past. Whatever their intentions, the dissenters were thus a source of scandal between the Church on the one side and the restless faithful on the other. The Church had accepted their presence in fact, but was not prepared explicitly to repudiate an image of its own place in society which held that their ascendance, if not their very presence in the new Spanish America, was intolerable. Meanwhile the faithful, increasingly less docile toward the teachings of the Church, urged it openly to accept what it had already accepted in fact, or to admit its solidarity with the past which, officially at any rate, independent Spanish America abominated. Rather than trying to guarantee the position of the dissenters, which had never been seriously threatened, they wished to protect themselves against any possible attempt by the Church to force on them the old religious discipline.

[40] Hamilton, *Travels,* I: 139–140.

Impiety among Catholics appeared thus to be as ineradicable a novelty as the presence of the dissenters themselves. Its advances were parallel to the increasing hostility displayed toward the Church as an institution. As far back as 1810 or 1825 large sectors of the population were already disillusioned with the capacity of the Church to adapt itself not only to the exigencies of the times but to those which it had always proclaimed valid. This substantially negative verdict only gradually generated a violent hatred among certain members of the population, to which they gave bent in far from rational terms. Zoological comparisons as uncomplimentary as those which the Stalin regime hurled at its adversaries during the grimmest period of the cold war sprouted from the pen of people like José María Samper of Nueva Granada, who was capable of greater serenity if not always greater perspicacity in discussing other matters. Militant incredulity partly grew in imitation of Catholic Europe, which was ill able to bear the weight of ideological and political restoration. (Precisely in Restoration France more than a million copies of the writings of Voltaire were put upon the market.) Even so, the local situation made some Latin American sectors particularly receptive to the European example. The doubts of José Manuel Restrepo concerning the beneficial consequences of expanding university education in Nueva Granada were not imperceptive. The expansion of university education was responsible for the multitude of young doctors and lawyers whom he describes as having "emerged from our schools and universities steeped in the utilitarian principles of Bentham."[41] Their superabundance and the excessive sarcasm of the criticisms, disrespectful even of that which was held most sacred, were closely related. Ostentatious insolence not only toward the accepted faith but also toward the "former patriots and the men who governed the Republic" typified after its fashion the impatience of the younger generation toward a Spanish America as incapable as it ever had been of ensuring them a chance to take over from the other. This being the case, the imported ideological

---

[41] J. M. Restrepo, *Diario político y militar,* June 25, 1845, III (Bogotá, 1954): 424.

arguments survived in part because they expressed conflicts embedded in the structure of Spanish American society which were due both to the crisis caused by independence and to earlier tensions which independence had not solved, in spite of the changes it had brought with it.

It was this unconnected and disjointed postrevolutionary situation which gave rise to the most serious political problems the new countries had to face. The dearly bought political wisdom which the leaders of the countries emerging from the emancipation struggle eventually acquired forgot the fiery hopes on which the emancipatory movement was born, and was content to live with problems which—as one sad experience after another apparently proved—it was impossible to solve.

4

TOWARD A POSTREVOLUTIONARY POLITICAL ORDER FOR SPANISH AMERICA

Given Spanish America's inability to find its own course, it is hardly surprising that Spanish American politics after the revolution should have reflected that uncertainty. There are any number of reasons for the fact that the theoretical solutions proposed for Spanish American political problems were not only varied and divergent but vitiated by internal contradictions. It had always been hard to adapt European doctrines to an entirely different context; now the intellectual disarray of postrevolutionary Europe after the defeat of the revolutionary movement of 1789 compounded the problem. This defeat was not only reflected in the new arrogance of counterrevolutionary doctrines which even the most conservative Spanish Americans could not accept wholeheartedly; it was, moreover, responsible in Europe for a reorientation of those who did not necessarily favor such doctrines but out of principle, or for tactical reasons, would not accept the compromising heritage of a Revolution whose outcome had been Napoleon's military despotism and was almost universally regarded as an enterprise turned criminal very shortly after its inception.

The intellectual elite of Spanish America, long used to receiving ideas from Europe, soon sensed the new European climate. Upon his return from Europe in 1816, following an unsuccessful diplomatic mission, the Argentine Manuel Belgrano brought back with him not only new ideas, but even a new taste in dress. The former revolutionary, who had dressed with Republican simplicity, was now a convinced monarchist who, even in the depths of the country, continued to dress "no less painstakingly than the most refined dandy."[1] Members of the Argentine Congress who in other

[1] J. M. Paz, *Memorias postumas,* I (Buenos Aires, 1948): 308.

assemblies before 1815 had addressed each other as "citizen" began to use the more neutral "señor."

But though revolutionary enthusiasm cooled quickly, independent Spanish America owed its very being to a revolution, and this doomed from the start the search for a *modus vivendi* with monarchist Europe. True, the actual plight of the new Spanish American countries was less desperate than they thought: weakened by war, continental Europe was in no condition to embark upon crusades abroad, and the new countries were protected further by the initially implicit and eventually explicit protection of Great Britain. Ideologically even more than materially the process of incorporation into the British ambit implied far less drastic alterations of the prerevolutionary order than had been anticipated. In Great Britain, Liberal trends were weak until 1830, and even later their best-known aspects in Spanish America were, from utilitarianism to free trade, those which sought to bring about change in areas other than politics. Charles Hale's remark that the success of Bentham's theories lay in their apolitical nature is applicable not merely to Mexico.[2]

This loyalty to a peculiar image of recent European history, based on the belief that the great revolution had been an essentially criminal enterprise, survived in Spanish America even when theoretical curiosity about doctrines proposing radical social change replaced the caution characteristic of the early postrevolutionary period. In Argentina Sarmiento boasted that the boldness of Fourier and Proudhon could not shock him, but it is significant that he, together with other enemies of the Rosas regime, could find no more damaging epithet for his government than to liken it to the Jacobins: Sarmiento was quick to draw the lesson implicit in the comparison by reminding his readers that the execution of Robespierre and "seventy illustrious miscreants" had sufficed to restore France to "docility and morality," thus putting an end to the massacre in which a million and a half French citizens had joined at the instigation of "those implacable terrorists."[3]

[2] C. A. Hale, *Mexican Liberalism* (New Haven, 1968), p. 154.
[3] D. F. Sarmiento, *Facundo, ed. A. Palcos* (Las Plata, 1938), p. 303.

True, the revolutionary origins of the European liberal democratic tradition were accepted shortly after Sarmiento penned his remarks, but this was due mainly to Lamartine, who idolized the Girondins as the victims, rather than the instigators, of revolutionary fervor. The American style of revolution began to appear more worthy of emulation than the French, stained by blood and crime, and comparisons with the "immortal Washington" became the favorite theme of journalists praising their governments, while the opposition muttered against taking his name in vain. The American Revolution, while unequivocally republican, scarcely appeared to be a revolution to those Latin American contemporaries who were unaware that it had roused any opposition among the local inhabitants. A partiality for the North American tradition is yet another example of the Spanish Americans' desire to justify their own political peculiarities. While they all favored free institutions and the majority continued to believe in the republican system in spite of repeated disappointments, they all denied the revolutionary content of their ideas.

Without a doubt Europe's distaste for its most recent revolutionary experiences contributed to determining this attitude on the part of the Spanish Americans, but its roots in Spanish American experience were perhaps more important. Spanish Americans had no need of European literature to become aware of the discomforts of disorder and violence. Their skepticism concerning the creative virtues of that disorder and that violence predates their reading the writings of counterrevolutionary authors in Europe and was born of intimate experience, which denied those virtues more vigorously than any theoretical treatise. True, in Spanish America violence and disorder were not necessarily linked with a revolutionary ideology, but precisely for this reason, the fact that disorder and violence were repudiated—and repudiated in the language first formulated with the French Revolution in mind—was less of a contradiction than is immediately apparent with the esteem accorded to political ideas and institutions which were, in the final instance, the fruit of revolution. Disapproval of the French Revolution symbolizes one facet of the complex Spanish American ambivalence—of simultaneous acceptance and rejection of its own revolution, too efficacious in destroying the old order, but less able to create a new one to take its place. While revolutionary violence and disorder were mainly condemned for their sterility, postrevolutionary violence and disorder were condemned not only for their political ineffectiveness but in a larger context as the main symptom of a repudiation of civilized standards that went beyond the realm of politics.

Denunciation of disorder, revolutionary or otherwise, was accompanied by a nostalgic longing for order that again was not merely of European origin. The biographies of any of the public and many of the private figures of those turbulent times reveal the immediate source of such nostalgia. San Martín decided to retire from public life to live on his country estates in Mendoza. His friend O'Higgins, exiled in Lima, approved his decision and felt that the choice of Mendoza was particularly fortunate, since its proximity to Chile would allow San Martín to "retire there should anarchy once again raise its head in the provinces of the Río de la Plata and from thence to Peru if the flames of discord were kindled yet again."[4] Thus O'Higgins felt that the serene retirement of his friend might well include two new and successive stages of exile. He himself wished for nothing better than to find a refuge in Britain, to enjoy a little peace at last, and would do so, he wrote, if he were able to rent his estates.[5]

Even obscurity was no guarantee against the consequences of discord. At the age of fourteen Domingo Faustino Sarmiento left his native province of San Juan for neighboring San Luis in the company of an uncle who had been exiled after taking part in an uprising against religious tolerance. At eighteen, together with his father, he sided with the party which had exiled his uncle, and defeat exiled him again, now to Chile and to a career rich in ups and downs. True, Sarmiento shared in the discomforts as well as the advantages of being related to the Oro clan, influential in the Church and in the Federal party of the western provinces, and his

---

[4] O'Higgins to San Martín, Lima, October 9, 1832, in *Archivo de don Bernardo O'Higgins,* IX (Santiago de Chile, 1951): 22.

[5] *Idem* to *idem,* Lima, August 9, 1823, *ibid.,* 4.

career was to be even more strongly affected by the influence of a father too easily attracted by the new opportunities which militant politics offered to the adventuresome. But, in small Spanish American cities what young man of respectable origin did not have family ties which embroiled him in politics?

A longing for order was born not only of the odiosity of factious persecutions which inevitably follow political tension and which made—in the words of Sarmiento—the old regime appear in retrospect to be free from violence and oppression, and the tutelage of the king be remembered as mild. Order was necessary for economic prosperity. While it would not be true to state that all those who had something to lose preferred peace under any political regime, for there were always some whose fortunes were so closely linked with the policy of one faction that they would have preferred universal ruin to defeat of their party, the collusion of such solid men of fortune with the authors of disorder was regarded with horror by their peers as a selfish betrayal of the common interest.

The first priority of any viable political program in postrevolutionary Spanish America had thus to be the construction of an order less likely to be disrupted by internal tensions. Unfortunately, unanimous nostalgia for order had a too telling counterpart in unanimous recognition of failure to achieve it. It was a long time before order was established, and the chorus of lamentations over its absence did nothing to hasten its coming. The very precise reasons for postrevolutionary instability listed in the preceding chapters need not be repeated, but the specifically political aspects to which that general instability gave rise and which any political solution had to deal with must be considered.

The principal aspect was, without a doubt, democratization. The principles of the people's sovereignty and of equality were accepted throughout Spanish America, but, as described earlier, significant departures from these general principles continued to take place. Slavery and the inequality of taxation in the form of the Indian tribute had as a strictly political counterpart the restrictions nearly everywhere placed upon voting. In some instances property was a requisite (as established in the constitution and laws of Gran

Colombia, although a trade or craft could take its place), in others —alternatively or concurrently—the ability to read and write, was required as in Gran Colombia and Peru. An even more efficient barrier against the danger implicit in enlarging the electoral franchise was indirect elections. Force of circumstance was bound, in small districts, however widespread the primary vote, to favor the appointment of local dignitaries. These representatives, although elected out of deference by almost all the adult male population, comprised an electoral body comparable to that which would have existed had the vote been restricted to the comparatively rich. Moreover, the problems brought about by the legal existence of a large franchise are not easily apparent to us today. Among the many ways of overthrowing the government practiced in postrevolutionary Spanish America, defeat at the polls was conspicuously absent.

In other words, the care taken to impose legal limitations on universal suffrage was superfluous. The political stability of Conservative Chile, which did not implement the restrictions imposed on the voting rights of the poor and the illiterate, as established in the 1833 constitution, is sufficient proof of it.

Thus the debate concerning the revolutionary and reactionary effects of universal suffrage appears in part irrelevant, even if it is interesting to note that a quarter of a century before Europe became aware of it, the Argentine constituents of 1824 realized that granting the vote to the rural population did not endanger the established order. The weakness of the vote as a source of power made its nature irrelevant: since the voters were called upon above all to legitimize a preexisting situation and had already learned that it was expedient to do so, in the last resort it made no difference what part of the population held this dubious privilege.

There was yet another reason, frequently mentioned to justify the merely nominal character of the electoral roots of political power in Spanish America. According to this theory, even the most extreme European restrictions on the right to vote did not do justice to the Spanish American situation, in which public spirit was deplorably lacking and where many of those whose right to vote would have been recognized even by the most restrictive legislation had neither the education nor the vocation necessary to use this basic political right. The imposition of solutions from above, ill-disguised by elections of predeterminate outcome, was justified according to this argument because it could not betray the wishes of the people, since these were nonexistent.

The conclusion appears to overlook some of the significant consequences of establishing a representative form of government. However limited the vote might be—by law and in fact—each election briefly but repeatedly extended the political body not only beyond the limits of the politically dominant groups, but even to sectors which the cautious doctrinaires of constitutionalism, struggling to survive in the essentially antidemocratic climate of the Restoration, would have liked to see deprived of any participation whatsoever in public affairs. Precisely because the role of the electors was essentially passive, Spanish American political practice, which continued to be conservative in intent, serenely overlooked the warnings of the doctrinaires. In Buenos Aires, between 1821 and 1824, the regime of Rodriguez and Rivadavia, which prided itself on its identification with the most powerful economic groups of the province, not only owed its existence to universal suffrage but made tactical use of the progressive increase in the number of effective voters. It organized urban plebeian support, even according a place in the legislative body to a "representative of the honored class of the artisans" who had acted as an efficient electoral organizer,[6] and made good use of the benevolence of the *hacendados* to impose a rigid electoral discipline on the inhabitants of country districts. When less direct methods threatened to yield no results, it even called upon the massive resources of the regular army to obtain victories which a more restricted number of voters might have perhaps rendered difficult.

The revolution undoubtedly had wrought very great changes in Buenos Aires, but even in Popayán, better able to resist change as

[6] Official letter from "Los Decididos," in *El Centinela,* December 29, 1822, printed in Republic of Argentina, Senate, *Biblioteca de Mayo* (Buenos Aires, 1960), vol. IX, p. 8279.

part of the solid south of Nueva Granada whose political and social conservatism Bolívar admired, the great Tomás Cipriano de Mosquera, while able to take political advantage of his origins in a society which paid deference to family tradition, found that he could maintain his advantage only by spending a considerable amount of his political energy on detailed attention to his electors. And although the inclusion of certain sectors of the populace in political activities may have begun by respecting the old stratified social pattern, the character of this participation soon changed. It was precisely in Popayán, whose social discipline was held up as an example to the whole of Gran Colombia as late as 1830, that the political struggles unleashed twenty years later in Nueva Granada most rapidly and finally acquired the characteristics of a social conflict, violent enough to horrify even the most extreme liberals of Bogotá.

The existence of a representative regime was not the only factor, or even the most important, in this far from irreversible process of democratization. Formal democratization, which so dimly reflected the effective equilibrium of political power in postrevolutionary Spanish America, was but one more aspect of a limited and ambiguous but no less real process of democratization of political life at every level. Militarization undoubtedly was one of the most important aspects of Spanish American politics, as seen earlier. Its potential dangers to whoever was in power, though recognized, could not always be checked. But the consequences of the wars of independence, which were at the same time civil wars, went far beyond militarization. Rival forces were obliged to seek support from increasingly wider sectors of society. In spite of the caution with which this support was sought, and among a multitude of unfulfilled promises, such as the complete emancipation of slaves, the abolition of the Indian tribute, and distribution of lands to veterans, it brought about less radical, but by no means inconsiderable changes in the caste system. Indirectly it created convictions and political attitudes in sectors of society which had not participated at all in public affairs in the past. True, an effort was made to transmit only those convictions least dangerous to the dominant order: the revolutionaries centered them in a new

American form of patriotism which implicitly admitted the legitimacy of leadership by a relatively small Creole elite who, with no particular desire to enlarge their ranks, nonetheless fought against Spain in the name of the whole of Spanish America. This brand of patriotism took hold outside the circle of the direct participants. To be sure, in some cases it was only in the form of a passive following which did not necessarily participate in the electoral struggle. In Buenos Aires, where fewer than 3,000 people had voted in the previous elections, in one day alone the state press sold 5,000 portraits of Admiral Brown, who in 1825 obtained unexpected victories against the squadrons of the Brazilian empire. This form of patriotism, employed to gain essentially passive support for the current regimes which identified themselves with the nation, was, however, far from affording a guarantee of unconditional backing. In Buenos Aires itself, a government like that of Rivadavia could appear to that malevolent but by no means obtuse observer, Lord Ponsonby, as "dominated by the wild spirit of the mob."[7] This qualification, which would have seemed absurd to Rivadavia's political adversaries, who accused him of being excessively oligarchic, quite accurately explains the motive of Rivadavia's vacillations in accepting peace without victory with the Brazilian empire. While victory was not essential to the dominant economic interests, capitulation would rouse the indignation of the people, whose enlightened leaders had led them to believe in the invincibility of the city of Buenos Aires.

It may be alleged that Buenos Aires, more closely associated with revolution than perhaps any other city in Spanish America (the revolutionary stronghold in Venezuela was located in marginal zones), offers an example too extreme to be typical, but even in very different contexts, the political consequences of democratization made themselves felt. In Valparaíso, where Captain Hall had been pained by the indifference of the lower classes to the passing of the colonial regime and the coming of Independence, by 1832 the governor, Diego Portales, organizer of Conservative

---

[7] Ponsonby to Canning, no. 23, October 20, 1826, PRO, F.O. 6/13, folio 114–115.

Chile, was displaying his respect for the changing humors of the plebeian masses in the case of the murders committed by a North American sailor who, struck suddenly with homicidal mania, killed four people before being overpowered. In the face of those who alleged that he was mad and hence not responsible for his actions, Portales preferred to consider him of sound mind and to have him executed. His decision was based not so much upon his assessment of the killer's state of mind as on his prognosis of the consequences of adopting any other attitude in the peculiar climate of Valparaíso. "It would be a lengthy business to tell you," he writes to his faithful Garfias, "of the declarations and conversations with which the populace express their opinions in public. The fight of a foreign sailor with one of our *rotos* could be enough to precipitate sudden disaster, such has the humor of the people become. All that is required is for one of them to raise his voice. As they know only the government, they blame it and say that foreigners have paid the culprit's weight in gold in order to save him . . . they say that they too know how to feign madness, etc."[8]

Following the upheaval which revolution and war signified even for Chile, even a conservative regime, which wanted nothing less than to be guided by the preferences of the masses, had to recognize that these preferences could not be ignored with impunity. Rather than witness an outburst of violence which it would have been hard to control, Portales preferred to sacrifice to the animosity of the people an assassin who may well have been out of his mind.

Turmoil in the cities was not essentially new. The old regime had already found it necessary to use the utmost caution in dealing with the populace, but the new order had more cause to fear trouble from the urban masses than the old. Authority was now more fragile, and its frailty more apparent to friend and foe alike. Above all, the formal process of democratization brought with it moments of political transition which periodically accentuated that very frailty.

[8] D. Portales to A. Garfias, Valparaíso, December 12, 1832, in D. Portales, *Epistolario,* II (Santiago de Chile, 1936) : 304–306.

The pressures which built up in sectors other than the elite of Spanish American society, from Caracas and Bogotá to Santiago de Chile and Buenos Aires, were nevertheless far from overwhelming. The urban disturbances which took place during the midcentury and marked the end of the period under discussion here made the elite more aware of the presence of alien plebeian groups, but they were not sufficient to break the predominance of the former in the political field. When the lower groups proved too serious a menace, as in Nueva Granada, they were suppressed or, as in Buenos Aires after the fall of Rosas, easily absorbed as an accessory and barely autonomous element into a political setup which they could not substantially influence or, as in Chile, treated with a mixture of repression and compromise. The indirect consequences of these external pressures were nonetheless important insofar as they affected the insecure internal equilibrium of the elite itself. It was from within the elite that there appeared the most dangerous threat to political stability. The incoherence and tensions of the ruling elite reflected the uncertainty of a continent which had lost its prerevolutionary stability and had not been able to reestablish it. The elite contributed with singular efficacy to perpetuating the unstable situation precisely because, whatever the changes which had taken place, they still wielded considerable political power.

Some of the tensions within the ruling elite were due to the peculiar characteristics of an independence achieved under the double influence of war and the opening up of foreign trade. The most significant was the emergence of leaders based in rural areas or, at any rate, far from the former centers of Spanish power. Attention has already been paid to the fact that the process of militarization brought about by war, which the postwar period was not always able to halt, was one of the causes of the success of these new men. The greater relative economic power of the rural areas, due to their increasing prosperity and to the decay of at least urban economies, has also to be taken into account. In Peru only the new prosperity of the guano industry, which included Lima and the coastal areas, was to mark the beginning of the end for the hegemony of the generals, frequently based in the southern highlands, whose quarrels had up until then filled the history of independent Peru: here it was the crisis of the urban and coastal economies the main source of the increased influence of those who set out to conquer political power with the support of previously marginal areas.

The city of Buenos Aires, which Rosas conquered from his country base in 1829 and again in 1833, was already prosperous. But the basis of its prosperity was to be found in the countryside, and this circumstance has some bearing on Rosas's success. At first glance his victory was due exclusively to his military superiority, derived from the devoted following he enjoyed in certain rural districts (which, in turn, at least in 1829, may have been due to the horror with which those rural areas regarded the brutality of the military group then in power in Buenos Aires). However, if his victory was well received by urban sectors other than the populace of Buenos Aires this was mainly due to Rosas's social background which reflected the new rural orientation of the Buenos Aires economic elite. All those who had something to lose could identify with this descendant of bureaucrats, married into a commercial family, who had made his fortune in the country together with so many other members of the political and mercantile elite of the capital. It was not only the rustic militia which was available to him which made Rosas's supporters in the city of Buenos Aires regard him as the "anchor" on which the stability of the city and the province depended, but also the part he played in the expansion of the rural economy on which urban prosperity increasingly depended.

It must be stressed again that those changes within the power structure of society, while cataclysmic to those who were swept aside, were almost invariably beneficial to local leaders who had enjoyed positions of power ever since colonial times. This is hardly surprising, since the ascendancy of previously marginal sectors of the elite was due to the developing prosperity of areas themselves formerly of secondary importance which had not suffered too deep a social upheaval. Less immediately comprehensible is the fact that this phenomenon should also have been observed when advancement was due to the changes wrought by war in the equilibrium of political-military mobilization of different areas. Since mobilization always implied the more active participation of large followings, a certain democratization in the leadership groups would appear to have been inevitable. But at the local, as well as at the urban, level, democratization was often more a question of political style than of the origins of the emergent leaders. Rosas attributed his success in the Río de la Plata to the careful attention which he paid to the humor of the people. Earlier on and for less exclusively tactical reasons, Artigas had tried even harder to identify with their aspirations. By birth neither man was considered marginal by the society on which he eventually imposed his rule. In this sense the figure of Páez is scarcely representative: his complete absorption into an elite to which he did not belong by birth, and which made him the founder of an oligarchic republic, contrasts with the vociferous, but not always sincere, professions of loyalty to the populace, made by other political leaders of less embarrassing social origins than the *llanero* leader.

This is not to say that the old elites took the postrevolutionary redistribution of power lightly on its strides. To those who suffered its consequences it signified the triumph of the plebeian or rustic barbarians. They would perhaps have been justified finding irrelevant the fact that from the viewpoint of those who continued to occupy the lowest levels of Spanish American society the new leaders had begun their ascent from quite high up the social scale.

The redistribution of power was not the elite's only cause for concern. Its insecurity had originated in tensions that preceded the revolution and which the revolution had intensified by giving greater political-administrative powers to new sectors of society. These tensions found two main ways of expression in rivalry between different families and generations. In colonial times the solidarity and rivalries of high-ranking families had been based on obtaining favors which only the Crown and its local representatives could dispense. Alliances between different families had frequently been brought about by the influence of a royal functionary who wished to form a local party. In Córdoba, for instance, as late as 1824, years after the fall of the colonial regime, Don Ambrosio Funes denounced the influence of a group of families which became allied under the aegis of that remarkable turn-of-the-century governor, the Marquis of Sobremonte. Sometimes a local party was already well entrenched when a Spanish dignitary found it prudent to throw in his lot with them.

In this independence introduced significant changes. While family solidarity lost none of its importance—the introduction of a political-ideological element made disagreements more frequent, but they never had been totally absent in the past—the relative power of the different families and the tactics which they employed to settle their rivalries underwent a change. Here too the consequences of militarization were felt. Wealth continued to be an important source of power, but it became more decisively so when allied to the ability to win the loyalty of large groups of people. In other words, landed wealth was now in a position to consolidate the advantages achieved over trade during the revolutionary period. At the same time, political fortunes, derived exclusively from public positions obtained through family prestige, became particularly vulnerable. The postrevolutionary fate of the Funes family in Córdoba clearly evinces this trait.[9] Its members were among the first to join the revolution, which, except for brief periods, favored them, but the impossibility of their continuing to trade with Peru, which had now been completely cut off, together with the loss of prestige and income from the high ecclesiastical and lay posts which had formerly been their independent basis of power, condemned them to progressive ruin and brought about the downfall even of their political influence. The likes of the Gutierrez family of Mendoza, whose protection of the Funes family eventually sought, came to the fore. The lands they owned not only protected them better against political vicissitudes, but gave them the valuable military support of their agricultural employees for emergencies.

Politically humbled and economically impoverished though they might be, the urban and Creole elite kept up their old rivalries.

[9] See the correspondence of Deán Funes, in residence in Buenos Aires, to his relatives in Córdoba, in *Archivo del Deán Gregorio Funes,* vols. I and II (Buenos Aires, 1944–1949).

The reduction of the spoils, more and more coveted owing to the general state of penury, served to increase internal tension, and the changing political style made it public knowledge. In Popayán, which Bolívar had held up as an example to more restless districts, the longstanding rivalry between the two most eminent families, the Mosqueras and the Arboledas, was given a new dimension by the introduction into it of a political element. The process which led Julio Arboleda, who fervently opposed the return of the Jesuits to Nueva Granada in the forties, to become a diehard conservative ever more interested in the Church during the fifties had complex motivations, but possibly he was not indifferent to the fact that the head of the rival clan was following the opposite course during the same period.

The creation of the daily press helped to aggravate the situation, the freedom given to the press allowing it to become the vehicle for personal controversies that were frequently insulting. In some countries, as in the Gran Colombia of Bolívar, the reading public consisted solely of the elite, but even there contumelies acquired a new dimension on being set in type. In a way, the tradition dated from the remote past: in colonial times disputes on matters of precedence between magistrates and corporations had been aired in the churches or in the main squares in the full presence of the public amid yells and abuse, and many disputes were prolonged by anonymous lampoons whose authorship was easily discernible. The stress on continuance of this tradition was not the greatest threat to the unity and stability of the dominant sector. Potentially, if not in fact, the daily papers were accessible to a reading public far wider than the urban elite. Even in parts of Colombia Bolívar could regard the freedom of the press as an incitement to social disorder, although he appears to have been concerned primarily with the prospect of the insolence of some all too prosperous *pardos* (whose advances it had already been hard to contain prior to 1810) rather than with that of the masses.

In Buenos Aires the dangers of the scandalous publicity given by the press to the internal conflicts of the elite were clearly perceived. Almost all the young of the city were literate, and in the countryside the *pulperos,* in their general stores, frequently read the newspapers aloud to their illiterate customers. Rosas, who at the beginning of his career identified himself with the elite, protested against the imprudence with which his political adversaries exhibited the more or less shameful secrets of certain of its members: social discipline, he stated, would gain nothing if members of the "foremost families of the country" who should receive the unanimous respect of their inferiors were publicly shown to have a propensity for accumulating rather than paying their debts, or conversely to be excessively thrifty or even immoderately filthy in their person or dress, or were conjectured to shroud the honor of their ladies.

This, then, was one of the consequences of a merely partial democratization of the political style, to which the elite with their internal rivalries were particularly ill-adapted: stripped, in more than one instance, of a political monopoly which was assumed by marginal sectors not altogether alien to it, the elite had no way of recovering lost ground. True, they were threatened by no new serious losses, since those who had now achieved the peaks of political power had no wish further to expand the politically influential sectors, but precisely because the new situation appeared to be relatively stable, they were not stimulated into developing that internal solidarity which external danger would have necessitated. They kept up labyrinthine rivalries whose danger was more clearly apparent to the beneficiaries of the recent modifications in the political equilibrium than to themselves.

Does this mean that the arguments whose sound and fury filled the daily press with a baffling mixture of ideological debate and gossip-ridden village dispute were only the continuance of family and political-administrative rivalries dating from far before independence? The researcher who despairs of tracing any continuity in the personal or political loyalties displayed throughout those interminable conflicts may be tempted to say yes, but it is a relevant fact that the emergence of explicit ideological-political alternatives lent a new dimension to the conflict. Furthermore, the generation gap in the elite sector itself was responsible for more durable tensions and allegiances.

Generational differences were also nothing new: a perspicacious observer such as Félix de Azara had remarked around 1800 upon the political dangers inherent in those sons of good family, all too prevalent in the cities of the Río de la Plata, who could find no appointment, or at least none to equal their ambitions. The takeover of one generation from another was particularly difficult in societies where the administrative and ecclesiastical structures did not always grow at the same rate as large families of the Creole elite and where a portion of those limited fruits of office, variable according to time and place, but always more considerable than some present-day researchers care to assume, went to old Spaniards.

The revolution appeared to fulfill the ambitions of the younger members of the elite in a manner as brutal as it was efficient. It not only snatched away the privileges of the Spaniards and Creoles who had benefited under the former regime or supported it, and increased opportunity by organizing a more complex military apparatus, but because its outcome was uncertain, it inhibited more than one of the well-established and mature members of the Creole elite, who preferred the relative security of a less important position, from participating. All this accounts for the spectacular careers of such leaders as Bolívar, the most famous of them all, who was so widely emulated both within and outside Colombia (Carlos Mode Alvear, who in the Río de la Plata attained supreme command before he was twenty-five, and the Carrera brothers in Chile are examples, but at a more modest level too, the revolutionary *cursus honorum* was covered with astonishing rapidity by less brilliant militants).

Once the wars were over, however, the situation changed abruptly. While not all the governments who owed their survival to the army were strong enough to reduce its strength, they could not afford to recruit more men, nor could they increase the number of government employees (although there were strictly local exceptions), and these had to resign themselves to seeing their modest demands placed second to the exigencies of the military budget. The most serious aspect of the situation, with regard to both military and civil appointments, was that by 1825 the generation which owed its success to the revolution was veteran in experience, but not in age.

Until the middle of the century all the Spanish American countries were governed by leaders who had already attained the heights of their military careers, or important political responsibilities, by the time the wars of independence were over.

At the end of the 1830s Juan Bautista Alberdi could write: "When our parents were twenty-five they had already liberated a whole world."[10] Those who were now thirty years old, Alberdi concluded, had failed to equal the precocious achievements of the preceding generation which would not hand over the reins. Was the younger generation to blame? In suggesting that this was the case, Alberdi was aware that his opinion would be regarded as paradoxical by the entire younger generation and that it was only superficially more acceptable to the older. What Alberdi proposed was that the former should abandon sterile arguments aimed at proving their superiority in favor of deeds which would allow them to snatch public leadership away from their elders.

Besides these young men who wanted to take over the government, there were others whose aspirations, while more humble, were not always easy to satisfy. We have already seen how Restrepo felt that the superabundance of new doctors in Bogotá was a political threat not because they wanted great careers but because they could not even "support themselves by practicing their professions."[11] Even if this invites the conclusion that resentment of the younger generation toward the older (as in the case of the tensions between different members of the urban elite) was again due in part to the fact that the limited posts were coveted by too many, the generational conflict had certain peculiarities of its own. Not only was the dividing line between the different generations far more distinct than it was in the labyrinthine conflicts between cliques and families of the elite; because the younger generation had been brought up in very different

[10] J. B. Alberdi, "La generación presente a la faz de la generación pasada," in *Escritos satiricos y de crítica literaria* (Buenos Aires, 1945), pp. 103 ff.

[11] J. M. Restrepo, *Diario político y militar,* October 31, 1838, III (Bogotá, 1954): 123.

circumstances from the elder, they also regarded matters from a different point of view. These circumstances gave greater strength and frequently authenticity to the political-ideological differences through which the generational conflict was expressed.

The different viewpoint of the younger generation was the more generalized characteristic of the two. Impatient to occupy the positions to which they felt they were entitled, the intellectual leaders of the new generation nevertheless evinced an unexpectedly deep affection and respect for their predecessors. The memoirs of the Chilean José Victoriano Lastarria, advocate of the new liberal generation of 1842, begin with a portrait of his venerated teacher, the learned Andrés Bello, legislator and poet, whose strong personality had set the cultural tone of the previous Conservative period. In the Río de la Plata the memoirs of Vicente Fidel López open less surprisingly, but perhaps not entirely irrelevantly, with an emotional evocation of his own father, the neoclassical and revolutionary bard of 1810 who had supervised his upbringing with such urgent affection. In a less personal context, the men of Lopez's generation condemned the "mindless sophists" who had broadcast the French empiricist philosophy throughout the Río de la Plata, but for Dr. Diego Alcorta, the most efficient of these sophists, they expressed a devotion so extreme that uncharitable observers found it slightly ludicrous.[12]

It was their merciless criticism of inherited ideas that gave unity to the protests of the younger generation. They directed their fire both against the prerevolutionary cultural and ideological tradition, most effectively continued by the Church during the Republican period, and against the growing conservatism of the former protagonists of the revolutionary period. They frequently attributed to the latter a sort of intellectual timidity at odds with their past political audacity. The resentment of the younger generation was increasingly expressed in the 1840s in the form of a liberal

---

[12] José V. Lastarria, "Recuerdos literarios," in *Obras completas,* X (Santiago, 1912); Vicente Fidel Lopez, "Autobiografía," in *La Biblioteca,* I (Buenos Aires, 1896): 325 ff.; E. Echeverría, *Obras,* I (Buenos Aires, 1875): 340–341.

renaissance of a very different hue from the first liberal wave, which after 1830 had given way almost everywhere to a definite conservative trend. The ambiguous relationship of the new liberal renaissance to the calamitous endeavors of the first liberal trend was examined with cruel precision by the Argentine generation of 1837, determined to keep its distance from the *unitarios* who had fought Rosas in the name of the glorious heritage of the previous decade. In a less explicit form this ambiguity was also apparent in the reticence with which the precocious leaders of the Liberal party in Nueva Granada (educated in the elite schools of the Conservative republic in Bogotá) regarded General José María Obando, who was for the liberal masses the epitome of an entire tradition of wars and sufferings, but who, precisely for this reason, so badly represented the new liberalism based not on factional tradition but on the desire profoundly to reform the way of living.

In undertaking a precise project of secularization and modernization the liberalism of the new generations paved the way to a different stage in Spanish American history in which the problems of maintaining a perpetually uncertain stability ceased to be as urgent as they had been during the quarter-century immediately following the wars of independence. But insofar as it proposed to limit the sphere of political power and to bring about a more energetic transformation of Spanish America, liberalism was for the moment condemned to occupy a marginal position in the opinion of a markedly conservative population. Taught by experience, public opinion believed that a strong government was necessary and wished above all to see that government secure stable internal order.

The Conservative tone characteristic of the most successful political trends was not in itself sufficient to ensure them total homogeneity. The discovery of a Conservative ideology was the result of a long process of blind search characterized primarily by an increasingly systematic pessimism, for which the European example was only indirectly responsible, its influence being mainly negative and favoring the loss of prestige of innovative ideologies but not the rise in favor of the reactionary ideologies which were found irrelevant to Spanish American problems. The first version of this Conservatism, as untimely and utopian as the Liberalism it opposed, proposed a kind of clandestine restoration of the *ancien régime;* admirably reflected in the final period of Bolívar, marked by increasing despair, it survived in the attempts at political reorganization launched in Peru and Bolivia by Andres de Santa Cruz, who very explicitly followed the tradition of Bolívar, and, less energetically, in the increasingly nostalgic tone adopted by Mexican Conservatism, as expressed by its most articulate spokesman, Lucas Alamán.

The increasing conservatism of Bolívar was based on an ever more open criticism of the revolution, which dwelled on the cruelty and mercilessness of its wars. Within the European context, humanitarian arguments had made the mere mention of war and death a political indictment against the revolution which had unleashed them. Bolívar deployed similar arguments to support a systematic policy of hostility to further changes following the pattern of those wrought by revolution: insofar as the cost of change in terms of human life and suffering was always hypothetically too high, change was universally and aprioristically condemned. Starting from that hypothesis, Bolívar's arguments followed, however, a more independent pattern: not only new progresses on the revolutionary path were unthinkable; even the maintenance of the equilibrium achieved by the end of the revolutionary period was impossible, since that unstable equilibrium constantly destroyed itself; the only possible alternative was then a more or less thorough restoration of the prerevolutionary political order.

This sad conclusion is, however, not inescapable even in the final stage of Bolívar's thought. From a letter to Santa Cruz, in which he exhorts him to avoid the "quixotic reforms" to which those "confounded congresses of foolish pedants" were addicted and to proceed "after the old Spanish custom, slowly and first seeing what is to be done," it is hard to envisage that he could have had any liking for drastic reform, whether directed to restoring the past or to drawing yet further from it, but it is a well-known fact that even at the end of his career Bolívar was full of ambitious projects of institutional reform.[13] His nostalgia for the colonial past is apparent not only in his ambition to restore order which had been battered down by revolution, but also in his more positive attempt at salvaging, at least partially, the political unity of the former Spanish empire. The difficulties in imposing his ambitious plans for a new order over the portion of Spanish America under his rule are well known. The precariously united Gran Colombia, which found it so difficult to keep political control of Peru and Bolivia, ended in failure and the Confederation of the Andes, which should have established more equalitarian relations between the former and the latter and loosened the close bonds between the countries included in Colombia was never more than a pious hope.

In elaborating political solutions (but not when facing immediate political problems) Bolívar seemed to suffer from an inability to perceive that certain changes brought about by the revolution were irrevocable. In this case change was due to the collapse of metropolitan power, which had maintained unity between the dominions largely by outside means. In other cases less noticeable and more complex transformation were also deliberately overlooked: thus the attempt of the Bolivian constitution to achieve statutory equilibrium between the power of the elite and the other social sectors failed to consider that no ingenious constitutional mechanism would suffice to correct the alterations which the place of the elite in society had undergone.

In surviving the merciless pressures of day-to-day politics, however, Bolívar displayed full awareness of the situation. In sacrificing in 1827 the political future of his Venezuelan friends (grateful though he was for their loyalty) to conciliate the rebellious military strong man Páez, and in deliberately breaking with Santander and through him with so great a part of the political apparatus which had been the backbone of Gran Colombia, he reveals that he was not unaware of the vigor of some of the new forces brought into being by the revolution, nor of the relative debility of others. At times it appears as if, in a fit of restrospective optimism, he

---

[13] Bolívar to A. San Cruz, Pasto, October 14, 1826, *Obras completas*, I (Havana, 1947): 1444.

imputes the responsibility for destroying the frail postrevolutionary order only to the crazy arrogance which he felt to be as much a part of the elite as their weakness. On May 31, while enumerating his supporters to José Fernández Madrid, he included among them "the whole of the Church, all the army, the immense majority of the people," and listed as his enemies merely "the madmen of Bogotá . . . and rebels everywhere."[14]

According to Bolívar's unexpectedly optimistic assessment of the conflict, only his own magnanimous determination not to reinitiate civil war under any circumstances saved his enemies from certain annihilation, but it is interesting to note that he arbitrarily omits mention of the essential reason why he relinquished the government of Colombia. He states that it was the obstinacy with which the citizens of Nueva Granada refused to approve his determination to repress the new Venezuelan insurrection once again led by Páez: since his policy of contemporizing with the leader of the *llaneros* did not prevent the latter from shaking off his tutelage, he prefers to disregard the insurrection itself. It is understandable that he should have preferred to depict himself as disdainfully handing over the reins to the ideologues whom he had always despised and who, he was certain, were bound to display once again their radical political ineptitude. It is equally understandable that he should have failed to mention the defection of the supporters whom he had accurately considered better ingrained in the postrevolutionary order, to whom he had granted privileged positions within his political structure, but who had dealt the most effective blows to the Bolivarian political systems.

Thus, for manifold reasons, Bolívar's account of the processes in which he took part neglects the peculiar influence of revolutionary and postrevolutionary militarization. Theoretically in favor of a Republican order, the stability of which was to have a solidly patrician basis, Bolívar was also perfectly aware that the hard-hit and divided postrevolutionary patricians provided with singular frequency the stimulus for instability. He sought the support of the

14 Bolívar to J. Fernández Madrid, May 31, 1830, *ibid.*, II: 884–885.

army as an emergency solution for this abnormal situation, without pausing to investigate whether this revolutionary offshoot would unconditionally support the kind of stability he favored. Nostalgia for an order based on obedience, rather than on the open threat of force (which he, together with so many other Spanish Americans, regarded as the basis of the establishment of the Spanish colony), made him indifferent to the possibility of building a new and different order, which would reflect the irreversible changes brought by revolution and war. Rather, he never abandoned hope that at some future point the elite would somehow discover the secret of internal harmony and the masses that of obedience. His confidence in the army's willingness to serve a policy aimed at bringing that day closer allowed him to await this development with equanimity.

It was not only nostalgia for certain aspects of the prerevolutionary past which prevented Bolívar from perceiving fully some of the dominant characteristics of the postrevolutionary situation. In spite of cruel disappointments, the political leader and revolutionary legislator could not abandon entirely the firm beliefs which had led him throughout his earlier career. More than one indication of this dichotomy is apparent, the most evident being perhaps his intense irritation at what he considered to be the chimeras of the ideologues, hardly in keeping with their quiet political style; perhaps Bolívar wished to drown with his rude protests the echo which their sentiments roused in himself. His rejection, justified on rational grounds but nevertheless highly emotional, of any monarchical solution was another—and not less clear—indication: it was not only that he, together with so many others, was convinced that an improvised monarchy could not be the depository of that traditional prestige which might perhaps make it the nucleus of a new political stability for Spanish America, but rather a moral repugnance for the institution itself, in which there survived something of his youthful indignation on seeing the French Revolution confiscated by Bonaparte. Revealing as his attitude is, it is not immediately relevant to the problems which he faced: his refusal to believe that a dictatorial solution could be other than temporary is far more so. Public freedom might be restricted and limited by law and even by events, but Bolívar could not conceive of a solution which would suppress it for good. Under such conditions, the only hope of long-term salvation lay in converting the ideologues to political common sense, and in this respect Bolívar's increasing exasperation toward them was due precisely to the fact that he could not make up his mind to force them to perpetual silence.

Failure was, to a certain extent, inherent in the project itself. Less securely supported than he felt himself to be by forces which he could not bring himself to use consistently, Bolívar faced an opposition which—as he forced himself to believe—had it discarded its crazy ideas, could well have become the firm basis of a more stable order. Because they perversely refused to alter their ideas and continued to oppose him, he revenged himself by imagining the future ruin their behavior would bring about. Images of social and racial war run riot in Bolívar's final letters. He foresaw that the failure of his political projects would provoke a major social catastrophe and considered that failure inevitable because Spanish America had refused to reconcile to the necessity of any form of order and had become permanently allied to anarchy and discord.

Bolívar's conservative ideas were no less utopian in that they denounced the utopian theories of the Spanish American reformers. Had Bolívar accepted the fundamental characteristics of the postrevolutionary period, he might have offered an answer to the postrevolutionary situation. As it was, nostalgia for the prerevolutionary order and loyalty to certain elements of the revolutionary heritage prevented him from doing that.

The situation was totally different from that of the prerevolutionary period. The fundamental outlines of a conservative policy had to be constructed around those elements of society which—strengthened by the revolutionary upheavals—nevertheless favored the emergence of a new stability and of course were not necessarily the same groups which had supported colonial stability. Did that conservative policy—so different from the restoration which Bolívar demanded—really exist? There are at least traces of it in those areas of Spanish America which, economically and socially speaking, had most successfully been able to cope with independence and full incorporation to world trade: in the Venezuela of Páez, in Conservative Chile, and in the Argentina of Rosas. Beyond those economically privileged countries it was also found, if only in the form of an ambition ignored by those who directed the political process, and it can be traced, for instance, throughout the labyrinthine, occasionally tedious, but frequently moving political diaries of José Manuel Restrepo of Nueva Granada.

The new conservatism was best achieved in Chile, not only, as Rosas observed, because democratization had been more limited and superficial than in the provinces of Río de la Plata, nor because the growing prosperity of new order failed to weaken the colonial elite and only gradually affected their internal equilibrium. The political success of Conservative Chile had also strictly political causes which were at least partly related to the well-adjusted political vision of its founder, Diego Portales.

Portales was an even more resolute conservative than the later Bolívar. While Bolívar found it hard to reconcile himself to Canning's death, which he considered an unexpected and possibly decisive obstacle to the progress of "the human gender . . . toward perfection," Portales for his part found Canning "too liberal." Portales' conservatism was possibly not entirely unrelated to the marginal position which he had adopted during the wars of independence, causing O'Higgins to accuse him of not having sacrificed anything "for our beloved land" and hence lacking "the right to rule."[15] It found classic expression in the celebrated formula according to which Chile remained united after weathering many storms thanks only to the "weight of darkness," the passivity of the population which not even the revolutionary crisis had managed to shatter and which had saved the country from terrible civil war. The formula reveals not only the limitations but also the inspiration of Portales's conservatism: even if it had saved Chile from a worse fate, passivity was not—in absolute terms—a positive quality. Portales's opposition to any too radical change not

---

[15] D. Portales to A. Garfias, April 17, 1832, *Epistolario,* II: 173; Bolívar to J. Fernández Madrid, November 13, 1827, *Obras completas,* II: 197.

only was not justified by unqualified approval of the situation which was being defended; it was perhaps more significant that it did not exclude the possibility—and desirability—of introducing greater changes in the future. This form of conservatism thus appeared, at least in part, to be an emergency solution for an emergency situation. Perhaps precisely for this reason it did not aim to give to the principles on which an order it was endeavoring to conserve was based greater coherence than that which they had gained from the confused process which brought it into being. There are no traces in Portales of that sort of restoration utopianism which at times appeared to animate Bolívar. He appears rather to have been simultaneously attracted by eclecticism and moderation.

This was apparent already in his attitude toward religion and the Church. True, Bolivar also had been fond of attributing firm resistance to secular measures to the strength of "superstition," and this at the very time when he intended to make use of this resistance to get rid of his political opponents. But the ease with which Portales referred not only to matters of ecclesiastical organization—even if his opinion that the main virtue of the clergy was their docility toward political power (provided that political power was in good hands) cannot be considered exceptional—and even more his feelings with regard to matters of faith reveal the extent to which his attitude toward the received faith was politically calculated. It is particularly interesting to see how Portales found in ecclesiastical policy the opportunity to proclaim his faith in the *juste milieu,* a principle from which he extracted corollaries which he found valid also in other fields.

Insofar as social equilibrium was concerned, Portales's position was one of moderation and stabilization. More than one contemporary observer, however, might have considered this definition inadequate and have felt that the merits of Conservative Chile consisted, rather than in its having achieved a certain balance between the classes, in its having assured the hegemony of one class over another. San Martín wrote in 1842 to Pedro Palazuelos that Chile had been "wise enough to maintain the barriers which separate the different classes of society, retaining the predominance of the instructed class who have something to lose."[16] But Portales thought otherwise. Other considerations apart, the restoration of a complete hegemony of what he liked to call the nobility would have been impossible. The examples of Canning and Wellington appeared to him entirely relevant to Chile, and while he thought that Canning had erred in tending "to place in the hands of the people instruments which they almost always abused and which in the majority of cases they did not know how to bear," he also stated that "Wellington wished to upset the stability of power by resorting to the opposite course, and such an opposition rose up against him that he was forced to return the seals of office" and that "the English had proved at last that lacking that equilibrium in which power is retained both in the hands of the nobility and of the people, the structure must topple." His careful verdict shows no nostalgia for a faith in the possibility of radically transforming the political body in the light of certain ideals.[17] But even if Portales did not deplore the impossibility of fulfilling entirely the principle of equality, but rather that of undoing the advances already made in that direction, he saw and accepted the changes which the revolution had introduced, both because he considered them irrevocable and because, implicitly but obviously, he regarded them as too limited entirely to destroy the robust colonial order. His pessimism was thus more qualified than that of Bolívar, for whom the only alternative to turning back was further progress toward chaos.

There can be no question of contrasting the sometimes hallucinatory pessimism of Bolívar with the lucidity of the founder of Conservative Chile. The differences between them are implicit in the roles they adopted in the process of Independence. Portales belonged entirely to the postwar period, and this period, although rich in strife and ruin, did not confirm the apocalyptic prognosis which Spanish America's political leaders so frequently made at the end of the war. The postrevolutionary order did include an

---

[16] J. de San Martín to Pedro Palazuelos, Gran Bourg, August 26, 1842, in *Archivo de O'Higgins,* IX: 124–126.

[17] Portales, *Epistolario,* II: 173n.15.

enormous margin of individual and collective disorder, both spontaneous and institutionalized, but—and this appears to be the secret of its paradoxical robustness—it had come to terms with the situation. In other words, postrevolutionary Spanish America was as much torn by tensions as it had been during the period of the wars, but these tensions no longer coalesced on the strongly polarized lines of the revolution. The "colored war," the wars between the American castes for the booty which their common victory over the metropolis had ensured them, were never to begin. While there was no lack of Indian uprisings and black disturbances (always regarded by observers who had not forgotten the fashionable prophecies of the thirties as the first sign of gruesome catastrophe) these events were not able to change the course of a political life dominated by the chaotic struggle between parties too prone to changing names and leaders, and less inclined to identify with well-defined ethnic and social groups.

Perhaps because of what could be termed its comparative irrelevance, the occasionally extreme violence which marked so great a part of this period in Spanish America had its obverse in a peaceful Creole gentleness, particularly attractive to foreign travelers who were only too aware of the more merciless side of the life which so appealed to them. In that gentleness were absorbed the contradictions which could not be resolved. When, in his imitation of Béranger's *Le curé du village,* the Peruvian poet Pardo y Aliaga recalled the gifts which the good village doctor received, he mentioned, together with the beer from the English merchant, the sweets which the nuns continued to make after the pattern of centuries.[18] As this Peruvian village, postrevolutionary Spanish America, more than resolving its contradictions, apparently had learned how to ignore them.

Even so, tension persisted, and whether it arose from passionate negation of a not completely lost faith in redemption through revolution, from a far less impassioned acceptance of the postrevolutionary situation, the Conservative solution proclaimed that a strong hand was necessary to cope with hard times. Did its

---

[18] Felipe Pardo y Aliaga, *Poesías* (Paris, 1898), p. 161.

supporters really believe that brutal necessity to be merely temporary? Bolívar for one did not. The Spanish Americans, "an abominable composite of those hunting tigers who came to America to spill its blood and to procreate with their victims' daughters before sacrificing them," were, he felt, incapable of redemption.[19] Rosas expressed his pessimism less grandiosely, and directed it at human nature in general rather than at the nature of the Spanish Americans. Páez, whose Conservative republic regarded itself as Liberal, may have believed it. Portales, who prepared an institutional structure capable of containing a transition toward other political forms once conservatism was played out, most probably did.

Sincere or not, Portales's diagnosis was accurate. Conservatism was the solution for a very specific Spanish America which had won its independence only to discover that the order which this process had made possible was unexpectedly static. The liberal hour was to strike in Latin America only in the middle of the century, when a new trend in the world economy brought the long-awaited changes closer, and even then it did not signify that liberty or equality became more universally respected or more widely realized than in the earlier period. It meant, above all, that it no longer seemed so essential to move slowly "in the old Spanish way."

[19] Bolívar to Santander, July 8, 1826, *Obras completas,* I: 1390.

SELECTED BIBLIOGRAPHY

Archivo de don Bernardo O'Higgins. 26 vols. Santiago de Chile, Archivo Nacional, Academia Chilena de la Historia and Instituto Geográfico Militar, 1946–1966.

Bazant, Jan. *Historia de la deuda exterior de Mexico.* Mexico, El Colegio de México, 1968.

Bolívar, Simón. *Obras completas.* Edited by Vicente Lecuna. 2 vols. Havana, Lex, 1947.

Bushnell, David. *The Santander Regime in Gran Colombia.* Newark, Del., University of Delaware Press, 1954.

Caldcleugh, Alexander. *Tarvels in South America during the Years 1819–20–21: Containing an Account of the Present State of Brazil, Buenos Aires and Chile.* 2 vols. London, J. Murray, 1825.

Calderón de la Barca, Frances E. I. *Life in Mexico during a Residence of Two Years in that Country.* London, New York, Dutton, n.d.

Codazzi, Augustín. *Resumen de la geografía de Venezuela* (reprint). Caracas, Escuela Tecnica Industrial, 1940.

Gilmore, Robert L. *Caudillism and Militarism in Venezuela, 1810–1910.* Athens, O., University of Ohio Press, 1964.

Graham, Maria. *Diario de una residencia en Chile.* Madrid, Editorial-América, 1916.

Hale, Charles A. *Mexican Liberalism in the Age of Mora, 1821–1853.* New Haven, London, Yale University Press, 1968.

Hall, Basil. *Extracts From a Journal, Written on the Coasts of Chile, Peru and Mexico in the Years 1820–1821–1822.* 2 vols. Edinburgh, A. Constable & Co., 1824.

Hamilton, John Potter. *Travels through the Interior Provinces of Colombia.* 2 vols. London, J. Murray, 1827.

Humphreys, R. A., ed. *British Consular Reports on the Trade and Politics of Latin America.* London, Royal Historical Society, Camden Third Series, vol. 63, 1940.

López Cámara, Francisco. *La estructura económica y social de Mexico en la epoca de la Reforma.* XXI, Mexico, Siglo, 1967.

MacCann, William. *Viaje a caballo por las provincias argentinas.* Translated by José Luis Busaniche, 2d ed. Buenos Aires, Imprenta Ferrari, 1939.

Miers, John. *Travels in Chile and La Plata, Including Accounts Respecting the Geography, Geology, Statistics, Government, Finances, Agriculture, Manners and Customs, and the Mining Operations in Chile.* 2 vols. London, Baldwin, Cradock and Joy, 1826.

Parish, Sir Woodbine. *Buenos Aires y las porvincias del Rio de la Plata, desde su descubrimiento y conquista por los Espanoles.* Translation augmented with notes and comments by Justo Maeso (reprint). Buenos Aires, Hachette, 1958.

Paz, General José María. *Memorias postumas.* Buenos Aires, 1948.

Peñaloza, Luis. *Historia economica de Bolivia.* 2 vols. La Paz, 1953–1954, n.p.

Portales, Diego. *Epistolario de don, 1821–1837.* Collected with notes by Ernesto de la Cruz with a prologue and new letters, some collected and annotated by Guillermo Feliu Cruz. 3 vols. Santiago de Chile, Universidad de Chile. Instituto Pedagógico, 1936–1937.

Restrepo, José Manuel. *Diario político y militar; memorias sobre los sucesos importantes de la época para servir a la historia de la Revolucion de Colombia y de la Nueva Granada, desde 1819 para adelante.* 4 vols. Bogotá, Imprenta Nacional, 1954.

Rippy, James Fred. *British Investments in Latin America, 1822–1949: A Case Study in the Operations of Private Enterprise in Retarded Regions.* Minneapolis, University of Minnesota Press, 1959.

Sánchez, Mariquita. *Recuerdos del Buenos Aires virreynal.* Buenos Aires, ENE Editorial, 1953.

Soetbeer, Adolf. *Edel-metall Produktion und Wertverhältnis zwischen Gold und Silber seit der Entdeckung Amerikas bis zur Gegenwart.* Gotha, J. Perthes, 1879.

Stephens, John Lloyd. *Incidents of Travel in Central America, Chiapas and Yucatan.* Edited by R. L. Predmore. 2 vols. New Brunswick, N.J., Rutgers University Press, 1949.

[Sutcliffe, Thomas.] *Sixteen Years in Chile and Peru, from 1822–1839: By the Retired Governor of Juan Fernandez.* London, Fisher, Son & Co., 1841.

Temple, Edmond. *Travels in Various Parts of Peru, Including a Year's Residence in Potosi.* London, H. Colburn and R. Bentley, 1830.

Toro, Fermín. "La doctrina conservador," vol. I, *Pensamiento político venezolano del siglo XIX.* Caracas, Presidencia de Venezuela, 1960.

Tristán, Flora. *Peregrinaciones de una paria.* Selection, prologue, and notes by Luis Alberto Sánchez. Santiago de Chile, Ercilla, 1941.

Tschudi, Johann Jakob von. *Testimonio del Perú, 1838–1842.* Lima, Consejo Económico Consultivo Suiza-Perú, 1966.

Vargas, Dr. José María. *Obras completas.* Vol. I. Caracas, Talleres Tipográficos "El Globo," 1958.

Veloz, Ramon. *Economia y finanzas de Venezuela desdc 1830 hasta 1944.* Caracas, Elite, 1945.

Ward, Sir Henry George. *Mexico in 1827.* 2 vols. London, H. Colburn, 1828.

Zavala, Lorenzo de. *Ensayo historico de las revoluciones de Mexico, desde 1808 hasta 1830.* 2 vols. Paris, Dupont et Laguionie; New York, Elliott & Palmer, 1831–1832.

INDEX